MW01076940

A Beginner's Guide to
SPIRITUALITY

*The Orthodox Path to
a Deeper Relationship with God*

by Father Michael Keiser

**CONCILIAR
PRESS**
Chesterton, Indiana

A BEGINNER'S GUIDE TO SPIRITUALITY
The Orthodox Path to a Deeper Relationship with God
© Copyright 2007 by Michael Keiser

All Rights Reserved

Published by   Conciliar Press
                A division of Conciliar Media Ministries
                P.O. Box 748
                Chesterton, IN 46304

Printed in the United States of America

ISBN 10: 1-888212-88-8
ISBN 13: 978-888212-88-4

Contents

Chapter 1

The Tender Trap

A personals ad appearing in our local paper recently read as follows: "Seeking single male under forty, attractive, *spiritual, not religious,* who likes theater, conversation, long walks on beaches." (Please note: I read this ad for research purposes only; please do not write or call.)

Spirituality is in! Monks can go platinum with recordings of chant, books on self-help spirituality hang on supermarket bookracks, while television mystics can teach you about releasing your inner spirit and being embraced, led, or stalked by the Light. And singles seeking someone make certain not to attract anyone overtly religious, but just the vaguely mystical; we would not want to discuss any specific beliefs when we could just wallow in feeling.

❧ *What Is Spirituality?* ❧

Spirituality refers to the practices and beliefs that individuals or groups hold with regard to their relationship to God—or the Divine, if that word is safer for you. It was not always so: in days of yore the word "spirituality" had an objective meaning that had little to do with the warm-fuzzy that tends to pass for spiritual life in today's market. In the fifth century we first encounter the Latin word *spiritualitas,* which referred to the quality of life imparted by the Holy Spirit to all who believe in Christ. There was an increased reflection upon the role of the Holy Spirit in our sanctification, and it began to be taught that the seven gifts of the Holy Spirit mentioned in the Old Testament (Isaiah 11:2–3) were specifically given to believers at baptism/confirmation, as were the gifts of the Spirit mentioned by St. Paul (1 Corinthians 12). Spirituality was an area of theological speculation.

During the Middle Ages the word "spirituality" was used in a variety of ways, but with a narrowing of application from broader theology to "spiritual life" or "spiritual exercises," so that by the twelfth century, "spiritual life" came to be seen as identical with interior religion and the devotional practices that fostered it. Later on, Christian writers began to use terms such as "ascetical theology" or "ascetic life." The Greek word *askesis* means to be in training, and asceticism, as we will see, meant something very active.

The word "spirituality" was formerly used in a specifically Christian sense, but today it is applied to all kinds of religious feelings and practices that are the opposite of Christian teaching. Practitioners of witchcraft like to talk about their spirituality, as if they were doing the same kind of thing that the desert fathers or St. Benedict's monks were doing; after all, it is all spirituality. The word has become devalued so much that there are authors who write on "spirituality and sex" or "spirituality and cooking." You can find books about the common spiritual link between Christianity and Buddhism, or yoga, or Yogi (Berra). It's all the same: as long as it is somehow spiritual, it matters little whether it is Christian or not; it's all the same God, isn't it? As the slogan goes, God is too big to be expressed by only one religion.

Spirituality has become linked in some minds with a posi-tive emotional response to something divine, so if you get your response saying the Jesus Prayer and I get mine by whale watching, this is all right, because it all works on some level. It is perhaps one of the greatest spiritual tragedies of the last thirty years that many Christians have assumed that to become involved in real spirituality, to experience something authentic, they had to go outside their own religious tradition—to one of the Eastern religions, for example. They had never been taught that the Christian tradition, both Eastern and Western, had such an experience. Given the lack of a clear, coherent teaching on spirituality, is it any wonder that many of the faithful find it all just a bit confusing? (I remember having to explain to my grandmother, many years ago, that Hare Krishna was really a movement, not a person named Harry Krishna.)

The result has been a tendency to color outside the lines, even for those who claim the name Christian. The following is from a book on Christian spirituality, written by a Christian, for Christians, in which the author relates the story of a friend of his who taught him the importance of hugging trees.

Suddenly, Monica walked over to a large tree, and put her arms around it. I was startled by this gesture and, hesitantly, asked her what she was doing. 'I am drawing energy from the tree,' she replied. I moved to where she was standing and asked her to explain this drawing of energy. She answered, 'When you are in need of extra courage for some difficult task in life, go to a sturdy tree and, intuitively, draw the strength that you need, let the energy of the tree push you towards your task; when you are sad or experiencing anguish, draw forth from a tree the consolation and comfort that you need.' I had always had a particular fascination for trees, sometimes even seeing them as symbols of myself, but finding a source of psychic energy in them was a revelation. (Max Oliva, SJ, *Free to Pray Free to Love*, Notre Dame, IN: Ave Maria Press, 1994, p. 125)

I am certain that it was. The author then goes on to relate that he now counsels people to "Be a tree, for example. Be a tree before God: listen to it, what are you saying to God? What is God saying to you? Or be a rock, a flower, the earth, etc." Or perhaps a fire hydrant; they have much in common with trees.

The problem is that this has passed from a Christian sense of spirituality—God can be seen in His creation—to a pagan one that misses the distinction between Creator and creation and gets wrapped up in egotism—the tree is a symbol for myself. This is the danger inherent in much of modern spirituality: it ceases to be a way of reaching out to God and becomes a method of focusing on myself.

Another contemporary danger is that spirituality becomes idealism—an attempt to create a fantasy world in which everything is perfect and holy, so we can hide away from all that falls short (such as that woman who falls asleep during the sermons every Sunday). We use our imaginations to make up an ideal world in which the messy way sinners act out in the Church can be avoided. In the ideal spiritual world, all the sermons are literate, all the young children well-behaved, and all the meetings orderly. It is a bit like hanging out with the elves in Rivendell. Unfortunately, this ideal world can become so important to us, so much preferred to the reality we encounter, that it becomes a way to flee reality, usually working itself out in a continuous round of church- or religion-shopping in which we never find satisfaction anywhere. We cannot, because the spiritual place we are looking for is not real.

❧ *The True Meaning of Spirituality* ❧

For Orthodox Christians, this is all just a bit much. At the risk of being accused of being tolerance-challenged, I admit I tend to gag at the misuse of a perfectly sound word like "spirituality." This word properly refers to the devotional practices that help us put the teachings of Jesus Christ into day-to-day use as we seek to learn God's will and then do it. You see, spirituality has a very practical purpose that has nothing to do with releasing our inner mystic; spirituality means the hard work of saving our souls and transforming the world. Genuine Christian spirituality has the purpose of keeping us focused, rooting us in the kind of incarnational religion that so many believing Christians seem to have wandered away from. ("Incarnation" is a theological word that means the God who made the creation actually became a part of His creation—became flesh as we are flesh. Christ became a real human person, just like you and me.)

Good spirituality keeps us balanced in our relationship with God, others, and the material world. Contrary to what some would have you believe, Christianity is a practical religion concerned with helping us overcome sin, draw closer to God, and become more like Him, so that we can bring others to Him. It has nothing to do with "pie in the sky by and by." Christianity is a materialistic religion in the sense that it is concerned about the entire material cosmos and its transformation. Orthodoxy is not about saving us *from* the world, but saving us *in* the world, using material things as a means for God to give us divine life and grace. The creation should be diaphanous; we should see the presence of the Kingdom through it, but it is always a solid reality.

Spirituality, therefore, is purposefully centered where we are. Even genuine mystics need to be concerned with seeking to know God's will in order to do it; otherwise they are just wrapped up in an emotional experience that ends in a kind of quietism. This might fulfill their personal needs, but is of little real use to anyone else. Orthodox spirituality deals with the practical living out of the gospel of Jesus Christ through practices such as prayer, fasting, almsgiving, and so forth, which Jesus taught His followers to do.

Spirituality creates a firm context within which to work out our salvation: the context of living in Christ's Body, His Church, building our lives on the foundations of worship, prayer, and sound doctrine. Genuine spirituality prevents us from wasting our time trying to reinvent the wheel of doctrine, so that we don't wander around trying to figure out what we are supposed to believe. Instead we can concentrate on the task at hand: growing in Christ so that we can "[find] out what is acceptable to the Lord" (Ephesians 5:10).

Use whatever word you wish: doctrine, teaching, or tradition, they are all important to a healthy spirituality. The traditional Orthodox teachings about the Holy Trinity, the Incarnation, and the Church make it possible for us to really know God. They are so important because what you believe about God is going to affect how you think about Him, and thinking wrongly can really mess up an attempt to develop any kind of relationship. Orthodox Christians are concerned about right believing, or correct doctrine, because we learned long ago that ignoring the directional signals leads us not to some kind of freedom, but to a colossal train wreck.

For example, many people today like to think of Jesus in very human terms, placing Him in all kinds of modern settings—what would Jesus drive, or would He work at Wal-Mart—supposedly in order to get a better handle on how to understand His teachings today. Do the Nativity scene in modern dress and pretend He is just living next door to us; take Him some cookies when He moves in. This results in a dandy heresy known as Arianism:

seeing Jesus as someone who is human enough, with some divine attributes, but not quite God. This heresy has been popular since the third century, and we slip into it all the time. The problem here is that a Jesus who isn't God can't really do much for us, other than invite us to barbeques and help us hang up the outdoor lights at Christmas. He certainly cannot save us; since he is not equal to the Father as God, he has no power to do so. If this kind of vision shapes your spirituality, it makes having a relationship with Christ somewhat silly and sentimental rather than saving.

On the other hand, perhaps you think of Jesus in another way, always looking at Him as if through a stained-glass window—a kind of spiritual shadow whose genuine humanity is difficult to accept. We don't think of Him as eating, or combing His hair, or doing any of those day-to-day human things He would have had to do if His taking of human life and flesh were real. Every time we say the Nicene Creed, we state that Jesus Christ was "incarnate of the Holy Spirit and the Virgin Mary, and became man"; but this remains an academic concept for many. This results in another mistake called Apollinarianism (this book will do wonders for your vocabulary). If the Jesus who shapes our spiritual vision is otherworldly and ephemeral, we are going to have a problem dealing with our own lives. As we wrestle with temptation and sin, what good will it do to pray to a Jesus whose humanity was so insipid that He never really had to deal with the prospect of falling? Only the real Christ of the full gospel, the God-man Jesus Christ, is going to save us, so we need to be focused correctly on who He is and what He has done.

❖ Spirituality and Religion ❖

What all of this comes down to is that spirituality cannot be separated from religion, although many would like to try. Orthodox Christian life cannot be divided from Orthodox Christian doctrine without going badly off the rails. In Christian living, fact precedes feeling if we are going to have any kind of healthy, robust relationship with God that results in spiritual growth. The reality of three Persons in one God, the unity of God and man in Jesus Christ, and the unity that exists between Christ and His Church are the solid foundation that makes it possible for us to change and grow closer to God. When we try to pull apart religion and spirituality, we fall into the tender trap of sentimentality, in which we never have to do anything inconvenient. This will neither save us nor help us grow morally, but will trap us in the netherworld of emotion and sweet feelings, where we worship our own ideas and congratulate ourselves on our maturity. That will be hell!

This does not mean there will be no movement or exploration in the spiritual life, but we are moving toward a specific reality within definite boundaries, so that we can explore what is truly real rather than just exercising our imaginations. Genuine, godly spirituality will bring us to a deeper understanding of God, ourselves, and our relationship with Him. We will see things that we should have seen before, understand ideas that we thought we knew but had only skated across the surface of. There is great risk in this, because as we learn to encounter God as He is, some of our pet assumptions about both God and the world will be challenged. We will have to lay some childish things aside. Our movement will be in directions we had not considered before, but always toward that which is sound and true. At the end of his poem "Little Gidding," one of the *Four Quartets*, T. S. Eliot sketches it for us:

> We shall not cease from exploration
> And the end of all our exploring
> Will be to arrive where we started
> And know the place for the first time.

Through the unknown, remembered gate
When the last of earth left to discover
Is that which was the beginning;
At the source of the longest river
The voice of the hidden waterfall
And the children in the apple-tree
Not known, because not looked for
But heard, half-heard, in the stillness
Between two waves of the sea.
Quick now, here, now, always—
A condition of complete simplicity
(Costing not less than everything)
And all shall be well and
All manner of thing shall be well
When the tongues of flame are in-folded
Into the crowned knot of fire
And the fire and the rose are one.

Chapter 2

Discipline and Training

One of the terms used to describe Orthodox spirituality is "asceticism." It comes from the Greek *askesis*, and as mentioned in the last chapter, actually describes the training of an athlete. The idea of training for the spiritual life is one that the apostle Paul refers to:

> Do you not know that those who run in a race all run, but one receives the prize? Run in such a way that you may obtain *it*. And everyone who competes *for the prize* is temperate in all things. Now they *do it* to obtain a perishable crown, but we *for* an imperishable *crown*. Therefore I run thus: not with uncertainty. Thus I fight: not as *one who* beats the air. But I discipline my body and bring it into subjection, lest, when I have preached to others, I myself should become disqualified. (1 Corinthians 9:24–27)

No athlete who competes seriously, whether for the Olympics or a weekend soccer team, does so without some kind of training to improve things such as strength and coordination. To compete without doing so is to invite injury and embarrassment. Lance Armstrong won the Tour de France bicycle race by riding miles every day. It is the only way to develop the necessary stamina to complete such a race. St. Paul uses the example of an athlete's training to make the point that a Christian trains spiritually to learn how to exercise faith and live in God's Kingdom. Of course, he says, we do not do this to win an earthly reward, the bottle of champagne awarded by a lovely woman, but a heavenly one—eternal life with God. And in this contest you do not have to come in first, second, or third in order to get one of the prizes; you simply have to compete to the best of your ability. Think of it as a Special Olympics for the spiritually challenged. God is very gracious to us.

To go into training for the spiritual contest, you have to establish a training regimen, deciding how much time each day you are going to set aside to work on this and what kind of exercises you are going to do. For our preparation, the exercises will consist of activities such as prayer, fasting, and meditation rather than wind sprints and sit-ups, but I can assure you they will not be any easier to do. Abba Agathon once described prayer as "warfare to the last breath," which is a pretty good description of the level of difficulty involved in our training. To coin a phrase, "No pain, no gain." (All right, it's not original, but it makes the point.)

The spiritual life is not for the timid or the lazy. The reality is that no athlete trains in order to reach a level of proficiency and stay there; the goal is continuously to improve one's performance, moving, as the Bible says, "from glory to glory" (2 Corinthians 3:18). In fact, a physical athlete may reach a level beyond which he cannot progress unless he resorts to some kind of drug usage; but in our case, there is no end to our growth in God. We will keep progressing if we continue in the effort.

✦ Finding a Trainer ✦

A good athlete has sense enough not to plan his own training; he hires a professional. You get a personal trainer to help focus your effort so you don't train inefficiently; that is what St. Paul meant by not fighting so as to beat the air. You need someone like that coach in the movie *Rocky* who kept throwing water in the boxer's face every time he sat in his corner. Just waving your arms around doesn't prepare you to box, but having someone who knows about it showing you what to do can prevent you from getting beaten to a pulp. In the spiritual contest, a training regime can be referred to as a rule of life or spiritual rule. Before you try to put together your personal rule, you need to consult someone who has experience in these things. Who you gonna call? Someone who knows something about the spiritual life.

At first you will probably turn to parish clergy. Most pastors would probably be happy to be questioned about something relating to spiritual life rather than the upcoming food festival. Most Orthodox pastors are already in the business of hearing their parishioners' confessions and dealing with basic questions about fasting, so they would logically be someone to talk to about developing a spiritual rule. However, your pastor may not be the one you will resort to as a spiritual guide over the long term.

There are several reasons for this. First, most parish clergy are generalists; they deal with Christian life in the many areas that come up in the Christian community we call the parish church. If yours is a large and busy church, they may not have the time to devote to the spiritual direction of a large group of people; even if they want to, there are only so many hours in the day. In addition, not everyone is good at everything; some priests are wonderful preachers, some are good administrators, and some are good directors. There is nothing wrong with acknowledging that spiritual direction may not be someone's particular gift. A mature pastor will admit that, and this means that experience does count for something.

If you are seeking someone to be a trainer for the long haul, you may not want to ask a young, newly ordained priest. Of course, I would not have said that when I was a young, newly ordained priest, but then I was a kid who thought I knew everything. I was wrong. New clergy come out of seminary with minds positively stuffed with all sorts of interesting and important information, much of which is absolutely useless for the pastoral ministry. You learn how to be a good pastor by working with people over the years, finding out how to do things right after you have done them wrong, and picking up the pieces. If you want help from someone in establishing a sound spiritual life, you might not want to ask someone who is still establishing his own. It is something to consider.

In addition, not all Orthodox priests have a blessing to hear confessions, and confession is an essential part of the spiritual life. As I have mentioned, the original sacramental person in the Christian community was the bishop; only after the fourth or fifth century was it usual for presbyters to serve the Divine Liturgy as a delegate for the bishop, and there was no blanket permission for them to be spiritual fathers. In some parts of the Orthodox world, it is still perhaps not the normal practice for all parish priests to be confessors. Traditionally, the role of a spiritual father was seen as being given to comparatively few—those who had the knowledge, experience, and perhaps most importantly, commitment to the spiritual life to fulfill the role.

St. Basil the Great wrote, "For he, who no longer lives after the flesh, but, being led by the Spirit of God, is called a son of God, is called spiritual." Perhaps there is a connection here with what St. Paul writes in 1 Corinthians: "He who is spiritual judges all things, yet he himself is *rightly* judged by no one" (2:15). I don't think the apostle uses "he who is spiritual" in the sense of some elitist super soul or guru. Rather he has in mind one committed to a vision of the spiritual life who has purified his soul and can see clearly what is according to the flesh and what is according to the spirit. This man is in a position to exercise sober, mature judgment when directing others, to discern their hurts and needs.

This need for discernment is the reason St. Gregory of Sinai gives for not granting a spiritual hunting license to everyone who wants one. "To guide others is not for everyone, but for those who have been given divine discernment, what is called by the Apostle, the 'discernment of spirits' (1 Corinthians 12:10), discerning the bad from the good by the sword of the Word." A genuine spiritual father is called by God rather than licensed by a board of directors.

Generally speaking, people who spend much time in prayer and fasting should be good guides to prayer and fasting: monastics, both male and female, are an obvious resource. Unfortunately, few Orthodox in North America or Western Europe live near a stable Orthodox monastery; if you do, thank God for it! It is worth the effort to search out a godly community and establish a relationship with its members, not just so that you can go and visit them, but so you can find a mentor and guide. Your ascetical trainer may be part of a team of spiritual "professionals" whose lives revolve around the prayer and worship of Christ's Church. Think of what it would be like to have as your sports mentor someone who played for an NFL team, who knew the sport intimately. In a sense, that is what it could be like to have a monastic as your ascetical guide. (My apology to all monastics for using the term "professional"; I only mean to indicate that they are committed to working continuously on the skills we need to live our spiritual lives.)

We live in an age of almost instant communication. In years past, faithful Christians who were not able to see their spiritual director as often as they liked would write letters, opening their souls and seeking advice. Many still do. But even on Mt. Athos there are computers, so communication doesn't take that long anymore. Problems that arise can be dealt with more quickly than ever before, sometimes before you can get a busy pastor's attention to ask a question. And if your pastor is your director, you may still be able to get him more quickly by email or cell phone than by waiting until Sunday morning. Think of what St. Paul could have done with a cell phone and fax machine.

Do not be afraid to consult any faithful Orthodox person who is serious about saying his or her prayers and confessing sins; many can be of great help in our spiritual struggle since they are walking the same walk. Not all saints are to be found in monasteries; there are some very holy people living in the world with the rest of us, exercising charismatic ministries. What is important is not priestly ordination but seeking purity of heart and striving to overcome the passions. If someone other than the ordained clergy, be they monastic or laity, does this, they may be able to bring someone to healing through their direction, and this is what is important. If the Holy Trinity is truly transforming someone, that person is an important resource for us.

St. Gregory of Sinai wrote about people who, while they may not be members of the hierarchical priesthood, have been illumined by the operation of grace within them. He writes, "A true sanctuary is a heart that has been freed from evil thoughts and receives the operation of the Spirit, for everything in the heart is said and done spiritually." Such people don't normally advertise themselves—if they did, it would be a sure sign they should be avoided—but word does get around. Ask others who are trying to grow in grace who might be of help, and I imagine you will find the help you need. One kind of person you should avoid, however, is the person who would seek you out, offering to guide, direct, or otherwise tell you how to live your life. Serious people do not do this. The person who thinks he or she is mature enough to tell you what to do may have a beam-and-mote problem of his or her very own.

✦ What Is a Spiritual Father? ✦

It is easy to use words loosely, and one that may cause a problem is the term "spiritual father." Certainly anyone who is serious about growing spiritually should be in communication with or under the direction of someone else who is experienced and mature—not perfect, but rooted in the Orthodox Tradition and able to deal with the problems and issues that will arise. This does not mean that you give up your freedom in order to be controlled. Jesus tells us to become perfect as His Father is perfect, but the Greek word used—*teleios*—means to act as maturely as possible. God has called us to become mature, faithful adults, and we do not become so by letting someone else run our existence for us.

Just because someone is ordained doesn't mean he has the qualifications to be a spiritual father. Certainly knowledge of the teachings and traditions of the Church is important, but so are other things as well. In fact, the term "spiritual father" can refer to priests who are functioning on various levels, including some who may have almost prophetic gifts, with an ability to see into the heart and know what is there almost without being told. People like this are somewhat rare; God does provide them when the world needs them, but you do not encounter them at every coffee hour.

Most of us who write and talk on spirituality are competent directors because we are trying to grow ourselves, to immerse ourselves in the life and in the study, and in that sense are spiritual fathers. I suppose the difference is that the first kind of spiritual father can point out exactly where you need to go, while the rest of us can walk with you and try to get there with you, because we are dealing with the same problems ourselves. Even the truly prophetic spiritual fathers function on the level they do because of continual ascetic effort.

I am not suggesting that we should not use the term "spiritual father," only that we need to understand what we mean by it. Ordination and education are not more important than purifying the heart in order to see God, and the ordained priest who is not really doing so is not a spiritual father.

The apostle John writes, "Beloved, do not believe every spirit, but test the spirits, whether they are of God; because many false prophets have gone out into the world" (1 John 4:1). One of the spiritual gifts we need to exercise is that of discernment. Just because something looks like a duck, walks like a duck, and quacks like a duck, it doesn't always follow that it is of God. If you are seeking someone to be a mentor or trainer, be careful. If someone seeks you out to give you direction, run; if someone wants to control your life by making all the decisions, run; if someone wants you to be guilt-ridden and intimidated rather than humble and repentant, run.

And if a relationship between you and the trainer doesn't seem to be working out, if you just don't get along and there is constant friction, there is nothing wrong with saying the situation is not working and seeking someone else. Just be careful you don't fall into the trap of shopping for an opinion every time you hear something uncomfortable. Never try to direct yourself; that is about as dangerous as learning to be an electrician by mail—someone needs to show you what wire *not* to touch. Be humble and teachable, and never be afraid to say that you do not understand or are confused. In training for the ascetic contest, communication and trust form the most important foundation.

✦ Setting Up a Rule ✦

Having established a relationship with your mentor, what kind of spiritual rule do you set up? The purpose of a rule is to be an aid to training, establishing certain times for certain activities so you can perform them in a focused, obedient, and efficient manner.

A good rule will cover things such as when you will pray and where. How closely will you keep the fasting rules of the Church, especially if you are new at it or have a medical problem? What kinds of financial offerings will you make, or how many weekly services will you try to attend? How will you prepare to receive Holy Communion, and how often will you communicate? All of these things you work out with your spiritual father or mother, and in obedience to the direction received, develop it into a framework within which you follow Christ each day.

At this point you will probably hear from some free spirit, "Aha, we knew it all along; you are oppressed by a religion of rules and you are not free!" Nonsense. Discipline and obedience have nothing to do with oppression; they have everything to do with taking godly life seriously. A person who obeys traffic laws is not free to drive in any manner he wants, regardless of who else is on the road; but he is not being oppressed, he is being kept safe. Nothing gets done in life unless we discipline ourselves to do it. If we are in school, we must study regularly; if we work, we need to show up on time. That is part of the rule by which we get through life in this world. Why would life in the Kingdom be any different?

If we care enough about God to take our relationship with Him seriously, we will plan our work, then work our plan. "For which of you, intending to build a tower, does not sit down first and count the cost, whether he has *enough* to finish *it*—lest, after he has laid the foundation, and is not able to finish, all who see it begin to mock him, saying, 'This man began to build and was not able to finish'" (Luke 14:28–30). We are building a life with God; this means we don't trust spiritual growth to chance and hope for the best, but give it our best effort.

A good spiritual rule will be invaluable, especially if it is rooted in sound spiritual tradition and practice, because that keeps us from wasting time trying to invent new and exotic ways to follow God. St. John Cassian wrote about the dangers both of seeking novelty and of working on your own: "We will most easily come to a precise knowledge of true discernment if we follow the paths of our elders," he writes, "if we do nothing novel, and if we do not presume to decide anything on the basis of our own private judgment. Instead let us in all things travel the road laid down for us by the tradition of our elders and by the goodness of their lives."

Of course, we still need to be discerning. A rule should be flexible, precisely because we are putting up a framework, not a prison. There is the danger that we will become obsessive about our discipline, forgetting that it is a tool rather than an end in itself. That is why we are under direction and should never try to work it out by ourselves. We might need to make adjustments; lives and schedules change, so that what was a good time and place to pray might no longer be so. Our physical condition may change, so that the amount of fasting might have to be adjusted. Or, wonder of wonders, we might grow spiritually stronger, in which case we could do even more!

There is nothing wrong with changing our rule to reflect changes in circumstances, as long as we do so in consultation with our trainer. Two heads are better than one, and we should never attempt to make decisions about where we are spiritually. The danger is that we may become obsessed about keeping our rule, no matter what; that we won't see the need for change, won't listen to advice, and will just plod onward, convinced that if we just try hard enough, it has to work. Frequently we feel more and more negative about our efforts. Trying to do the same thing over and over, with the same bad result, is a good definition of madness. This is why we humbly sit down with someone else and talk about what is happening and why. If we do wind up worshipping the rules rather than God, we are in trouble.

Chapter 3

The Three-Legged Stool

Three elements provide the foundation for any serious Orthodox spiritual life: the Divine Liturgy, the daily worship of the Church, and personal prayer. Any good rule will focus on these parts of spiritual life, keeping them in proper balance. Think of them as the legs on a stool: the stool is perfectly safe and stable if it has at least three legs to support itself and whatever weight is placed on it; but if you remove one of the legs, the stool will collapse and anyone sitting on it will fall. If we try to live spiritual lives that do not have these three legs, they will collapse. (I promise to stop beating this particular image to death.)

✦ *The Divine Liturgy* ✦

The Divine Liturgy is at the center of the Church's being. While Orthodox devotion does not generally focus on body parts, such as the Sacred Heart of the Roman tradition, I think it would be appropriate to call the Divine Liturgy the heartbeat of Christ's Body. Not just the offering of the Divine Liturgy, but also a prepared reception of the Holy Eucharist, the Body and Blood of Jesus Christ, is of absolute importance based on the teaching of the Lord: "Unless you eat the flesh of the Son of Man and drink His blood, you have no life in you" (John 6:53). The opposite of life is death, so if we have no life in us without Holy Communion we are spiritually dead, no matter what else we are doing. We can fast, pray, and make prostrations until the cows come home, but without participation in the Divine Liturgy we are simply spiritual zombies, the walking dead in Christ.

What really happens when we offer the Divine Liturgy? Is it a show, a spiritual play, something acted out for our edification? What is it that Jesus started at the Last Supper that we continue today? When we gather to offer the Divine Liturgy, we come together to be the fullness of the Body of Christ in whatever place we happen to be offering it. Obviously this does not mean that all Orthodox Christians in the world gather in one spot, but when the congregation of clergy and people come together, that is the complete expression of Christ's Body in that place. The late Fr. Alexander Schmemann wrote in his book, *The Eucharist*:

> The Liturgy is the "sacrament of the assembly." Christ came to "gather into one the children of God who were scattered abroad" (Jn. 11:52), and from the very beginning the Eucharist was a manifestation and realization of the unity of the new people of God, gathered by Christ and in Christ. We need to be thoroughly aware that we come to the temple not for individual prayer but to *assemble together as the Church*, and the visible temple itself is but an image of the temple not made by hands.

We are gathered by Christ and in Christ; we come together to be with Him and of Him. To say that we are "going to church" is a profound statement of what Christian life is supposed to be—centered and focused on Jesus Christ, eating and drinking with Him at His table in His Kingdom. To say that we are going to church means that we are going to show the world all the holiness and perfection of God as we worship Him. We do not gather as a collection of isolated persons who happen to encounter each other as we separately make our way toward God; we gather as members of one living organism called the Body of Christ. "Now you are the body of Christ, and members individually," St. Paul teaches us (1 Corinthians 12:27). There is no Lone Ranger in the Christian religion, no one who is an island unto himself; the Orthodox Christian faith is the religion of a community of people.

We become members of this Body when we are joined to Christ in baptism, but it is when we come together and offer the Eucharist that we become one with each other. Again, St. Paul is very direct in his teaching: "For we, *though* many, are one bread *and* one body; for we all partake of that one bread" (1 Corinthians 10:17). Because we share a common faith culminating in the eucharistic offering of the Divine Liturgy, and because we partake of the gifts of Holy Communion, we are made into one Body.

And there is really only one Liturgy: that which is offered in heaven by the ascended Lord. Each community that offers the Liturgy, whenever and wherever this happens, enters into and becomes one with the heavenly offering Jesus makes. "For Christ has not entered the holy places made with hands, *which are* copies of the true, but into heaven itself, now to appear in the presence of God for us" (Hebrews 9:24). For this reason, the Holy Eucharist is the center of focus and action in the Church; it is the beating of its heart.

✦ *Personal Prayer* ✦

So far so good. Orthodox and many other Christians recognize the centrality of the Eucharist in their lives, even if they do not grasp all the details of why it is so important; even an increasing number of Protestant communities have adopted a Eucharist-centered worship. Likewise, few Christians of any stripe would underestimate the importance of prayer, even if they personally pray very little. Perhaps part of the reason for not praying much is that we sometimes have some very odd ideas about what prayer is and what it does. If we have no direction in the matter, the attitude might be to pray infrequently, perhaps not so much to avoid mistakes as to avoid disappointment.

> . . . And prayer is more
> Than an order of words, the conscious occupation
> Of the praying mind, or the sound of the voice praying.
> And what the dead had no speech for, when living,
> They can tell you, being dead: the communication
> Of the dead is tongued with fire beyond the language of the
>   living. (T. S. Eliot, "Little Gidding," *Four Quartets*)

Prayer is conversation with God, learning about God, and remembering God. As an act it is beyond the ability of no one; anyone who can speak and think can pray. No great learning is required in order to pray, and fortunately you don't have to be a saint; but you do need to have a desire for God. Prayer requires an act of will; we must make a decision to pray and struggle with the problems of perseverance and distraction that will occur. If you only pray when you feel like it, you will pray very little.

At its most basic, prayer is talking to God in simple, direct, and clear language. It is not necessary to use fancy words to impress God with either our piety or our vocabulary. Speaking from your heart is the best way to go about it: glorifying Him for being the source of life, which is adoration; asking for our needs to be met, which is petition; asking help for others, which is intercession; speaking words of gratitude for the blessings we have been given, which is thanksgiving. All those kinds of prayer should be part of how we talk to God in a balanced, healthy way.

Learning to have a balanced prayer life—by which I mean keeping the emphasis off ourselves and focusing it on God—is the reason we often begin with prayers that have been used by many others before us. Jesus taught His own disciples to do this when He gave them the Lord's Prayer as an instructional guide to praying. There is nothing wrong with using written prayers from a book to get ourselves going and to help us keep our focus in prayer, especially if we are having trouble finding words. Certainly the ideal is to pray in our own words, but our own words can become self-centered, self-serving, and, let's be honest, a bit vague.

The Lord's Prayer and other well-written prayers start by praising God and then move on to other matters. They provide the springboard for our own efforts, keep us focused in sound teaching, and prevent us from wandering off into egocentrism. Such prayers are in the truest sense a manifestation of the Tradition: that which is handed on. We are not the first people to pray, and our prayers, although uniquely our own, are still part of the great river of Christian experience that flows down from the Incarnation to our day. "There is nothing new under the sun," we read in Ecclesiastes—what we deal with in our relationship with God is not different from what the saints and ordinary Christians who have gone before us have dealt with. We can profit from their example.

We learn about God in prayer precisely because we talk to Him. The surest way to get to know anyone is to spend time with that person, focusing on him and speaking with him. This is how it works in human relationships with our friends and loved ones, and this is how it works in a relationship with God. So many people know so little of God because they spend no time in prayer. It is hard to know someone you share nothing with, and talking is part of the sharing. We may not even mean to share thoughts and feelings directly, but as we talk we let little bits of ourselves out for others to encounter by the way we emphasize a phrase or the expression we have when we speak.

If we allow prayer to be a dialogue in which we actually listen for God to share and communicate with us, we can learn about His love, goodness, and holiness because He will convey these things to us, not so much in words, but by encounter and action. I have rarely heard God speak to me in words, but I have often had a confirmation of feeling or a sense of shared love. Heart can touch heart, and when God touches our heart, which is the reasoning, communicating part of our soul, we learn of His will for us in matters great and small.

Prayer is also remembering God in the real sense of the word "remembrance." In the Divine Liturgy the celebrant recites Jesus' words at the Last Supper: "Do this in remembrance of Me" (Luke 22:19). In Greek the word translated "remembrance" means to recall or bring back among us. When the words are done, when we have asked what we can and prayed for whom we will, when we have praised and adored to the best of our ability, when we have used up all the words we have, there is just the encounter with God. On a higher level even than sharing and learning, there is a level of contemplation that is the experience of God's being and presence, insofar as we can receive it—not experienced in images or comprehension, but more in terms of heart touching heart. For most of us this may be a rare experience. For those who have made the spiritual journey with faith and persistence for many years, who have purified their hearts and centered themselves in the life of the Holy Trinity, it may be the level on which they normally pray—for that is the way in which the Persons of the Trinity, Father, Son, and Holy Spirit, encounter each other. This is prayer at its most profound.

In a work entitled *The Incomprehensibility of God*, St. Gregory of Nyssa writes of something like this:

Night designates the contemplation of invisible things after the manner of Moses who entered into the darkness where God was, this God who makes of darkness His hiding place. Surrounded by the divine night of the soul she seeks Him who is hidden in darkness. She possesses indeed the love of Him whom she seeks, but the Beloved escapes the grasp of her thoughts.

Remember also that although we must choose to pray, that does not mean the prayer is only the result of our own effort. It is God who empowers us to seek and to pray by the grace of His Holy Spirit. As St. Paul writes in Romans, "Likewise the Spirit also helps in our weaknesses. For we do not know what we should pray for as we ought, but the Spirit Himself makes intercession for us with groanings which cannot be uttered. Now He who searches the hearts knows what the mind of the Spirit is, because He makes intercession for the saints according to the will of God" (Romans 8:26–27). Prayer is a cooperative effort between the Holy Spirit and ourselves, and the Spirit will guide and direct our effort if we open up to God. "God gives prayer to the man who prays," St. John Climacus teaches. If we give ourselves over to the act of prayer with faith and perseverance, prayer will come.

✦ Daily Worship ✦

In addition to our private prayer, there is a corporate prayer of the Church that is offered to God each day. We are familiar with the corporate worship in the Divine Liturgy, but additional services are offered to God throughout every day that are an important part of the Orthodox Church's cycle of worship. This is the third leg of our stool that represents the balanced life of worship and prayer that should be normal.

This leg is perhaps the least known to many Orthodox

Christians. Daily worship is not just for monastics. If we are active in our local parish, we may at least know that in addition to the Divine Liturgy, there are the services that are linked with the Liturgy and are meant to be offered along with it in the parish cycle of worship: Vespers and Matins. Vespers is the service that sanctifies the coming of evening, and Matins the coming of morning. In many Orthodox churches, Vespers is served on Saturday night and Matins on Sunday morning, or Vespers and Matins may be combined on Saturday night; but both of these services are linked to the theme of worship of each Sunday and complement the hymns and readings of the Divine Liturgy. The services are rooted in the Psalter, which was the hymnbook of the early Church, as well as in the later-developing hymns and canons that express our faith. This material teaches about the feasts, fasts, and lives of the saints, and attending these services is an excellent way to prepare for Sunday's Divine Liturgy, especially if you are going to receive Holy Communion.

Other services, however, have developed throughout the centuries, possibly originating in the private devotions of Christians but later developing into corporate liturgical services. The famous Bible scholar Jerome once wrote, "Who is it that does not know the ordinary hours of prayer to be the third, the sixth, and the ninth, together with the morning and the evening." He is likely referring to the times that Christians were expected to pray privately or sing the psalms, but this practice provided the basis on which liturgical services developed that sanctified the passing of the day. These came to be called the Hours. In the way we count time, this came to mean prayers at six A.M., nine A.M., noon, and three P.M., in addition to Matins and Vespers. Another service, which took place just before sleep, was called Compline.

Remember that in the time of the early Church, people lived by the sun, getting up and going to sleep earlier than we tend to do today. Vespers may have been offered any time between three and four P.M., with Compline and bedtime coming at about eight P.M. The full round of services probably only took place in monasteries and large cathedrals, and there is plenty of evidence that the local Christian population attended those services when they could.

Today most of us do not live near a monastery where these services are offered, and many churches may only have Vespers and Matins once a week. If you are fortunate to belong to a congregation where more of the daily round of services is offered, thank God for that and attend when you can. If these are not available to you, there are things you can do on your own. Several published editions of the Hours are available which you can use on your own. The structure of the Hours is simple, with few changes even during Lent, so you can offer them to God without worrying about juggling too many books. The services consist of psalms, hymns, and prayers, and if you don't know the proper tunes for the psalms and hymns, don't worry about it; simply chant them in a monotone.

The services of Vespers and Matins are much more complicated and can be a bit intimidating, even to those who have experience with them, but this need not prevent you from using parts of them. The Psalter, which was the first hymnbook of the Christian Church, has been divided up into sections called *kathisma* just so they can be offered during Matins and Vespers. You may look up the psalms for the day in any of several service books. Ask your pastor or someone more experienced in these things to help you. It is possible to get a Psalter already divided up for you: the one published by Holy Transfiguration Monastery in Brookline, Massachusetts, comes to mind. You may chant the psalms for each day along with the *apolytikia* (hymns) for the day, and by using an Orthodox calendar, get the daily epistle and

Gospel readings. This will keep you busy if you make it a part of your rule, offering it along with your own prayers.

We do this because the continual cycle of diurnal worship focuses us on God through the passage of the day. It keeps us from becoming completely fixated on the circumstances of our life with its problems and complexities to the extent that we see nothing else, and refers that life to God. Because whether these services are being done by a large group on Mt. Athos or a small group in Dayton, or just by ourselves in our prayer corner, we are joined in a corporate offering made by the Church on behalf of the entire Body.

As at the Divine Liturgy of St. Basil we pray for those who are absent for "reasonable cause," offering the Liturgy for them, so when we pray these daily prayer services of the Church, we make an offering for all those who either are unaware of the need to pray or whose circumstances may make it impossible to pray. We join in the worship of the entire Body. Even if we are chanting our psalms alone, this makes our effort stronger by joining it to that of the larger worshipping community. Additionally, these daily services of the Church give us a heavy dose of Scripture, with the psalms and daily readings that keep us focused on the mind of the Church as revealed in the Bible. Combine that with the doctrine expressed in the various hymns, and it becomes rather difficult to wander off the theological reservation unless you are really determined to make the trip.

The three-legged stool of the spiritual tradition—the Divine Liturgy, personal prayer, and daily worship—will be the foundation of your spiritual efforts. As you and your spiritual father develop your spiritual discipline, examine it in the light of these elements to keep it balanced, whole, and sane.

Chapter 4

Kinds of Prayer

S t. John of Damascus defines prayer as "the lifting up of the mind to God." Ordinarily our minds are occupied with all kinds of matters that have nothing to do with God. When we pray, we deliberately try to put these things aside, "laying aside all earthly cares" as we "lift up our hearts" (if I may borrow language from the Divine Liturgy). We are trying to lift our minds above the visible creation, even above the angels and the saints, to God Himself. There is more involved than just "saying our prayers"; we are trying to be in communion with God and to learn His will for us.

Understanding what kind of prayer we are offering is important to establishing a nourishing relationship with God. I have alluded to the fact that several different kinds of prayer are necessary to a balanced and healthy spiritual life. Let us examine these to see how the pieces fit together. Understand that the action of prayer may vary with the individual or the circumstances, but the essence of our praying is always "the lifting up of the mind to God."

We may identify four kinds of prayer: adoration, thanksgiving, penitence, and petition.

✦ *Adoration* ✦

Adoration is recognizing God for who He is, and the language of adoration is most often linked with the Church's worship of Him. When the prophet Isaiah had a vision of God in the temple, he responded by writing, "Woe *is* me, for I am undone! / Because I *am* a man of unclean lips, / And I dwell in the midst of a people of unclean lips; / For my eyes have seen the King, / The LORD of hosts" (Isaiah 6:5). Our growth in holiness will begin with two visions: the first is of God, transcendent and glorious beyond anything we can imagine; and the second is of ourselves in relation to that glorious majesty. In short, we need to see that (1) there is a God; and (2) we are not He. The act of praying is not always about us.

Adoration is the natural response of the creature in the presence of its Creator. God is our King and Lord, our Father who has adopted us into His family by grace and has surrounded us with endless compassion and love. He is the transcendent Creator of the universe, who by means of the Incarnation of His Son Jesus, who joins heaven and earth together in Himself, allows us a relationship of great intimacy. There is always an element of respect in any true form of love, and with our love for God that respect comes out as adoration. When we pray, we do so as children in our Father's house, but also as servants before the great King. Christ has humbled Himself to enter into the creation and death on the Cross so that we might be restored to our true home; but we are very unworthy of this. If we forget this, our intimacy with God, rather than being the familiar relationship of the faithful servant with his Lord, may easily turn into the familiar contempt of one who believes he is entitled to a response, no matter what. God loves us and desires to give to us both Himself and those gifts that are necessary for our salvation—not because we are worthy, but because He is gracious and good.

When we pray, we need to remember whose presence we are in and love Him for Himself, rather than for the things we receive from Him. We praise Him for His mighty acts, such as the Creation, the Incarnation, and other saving acts: "the Cross, the grave, the Resurrection on the third day, the Ascension into heaven, the sitting at the right hand, and the second and glorious Coming." Remembering these specific actions in the history of our salvation can be especially helpful when we are less sensitive to God in our surroundings than we should be. Many there are who can sense God in the glow of the sunset, and when they do are moved to adoration; others are transported by music in the same way. But for those who only see filtered light or a clump of notes on a page, those actions of God that result in our salvation give us plenty of reason to glorify Him. However you manage it, adoration is the fundamental act of prayer for the soul that truly knows God.

✦ *Thanksgiving* ✦

Thanksgiving flows naturally from adoration, because we are thanking God for being God and rejoicing that we are in His presence. You might almost say that we are thanking Him that He is. Obviously there would be a strong connection between thinking of God's mighty acts, adoring Him because of them, and actually thanking Him for having done them. I suppose it would be possible to do the one without the other, but what would be the point? When someone hands you a gift, you normally thank them right after the act of giving, rather than postponing it until some other time. You could, of course, just bask in the moment of the giving, contemplating the other's actions of choosing the gift and transporting it to you as things in themselves, but unless you say "Thank you," the giver might think you just a bit rude and narcissistic.

The list of things we could thank God for is a very long one indeed: we thank Him for Himself; for His mercy, love, and grace; for the Sacraments; for Jesus' Incarnation; for the giving of the Holy Spirit; for the life of the Holy Trinity—the list goes on and on. I believe that our thanking God for these things is very precious to Him, representing as it does a real understanding on the part of His children of what has been accomplished for them. In addition, thanking God for these things makes them more real to us, making of them not just doctrines or ideas that we assent to, but genuine acts of love that have moved us to gratitude.

And yet my pastoral experience is that thanksgiving, as such, forms a small part of the regular prayers of most Christians, even when they have received an obvious answer to prayer. Jesus had just such an encounter:

Now it happened as He went to Jerusalem that He passed through the midst of Samaria and Galilee. Then as He entered a certain village, there met Him ten men who were lepers, who stood afar off. And they lifted up their voices and said, "Jesus, Master, have mercy on us!"

So when He saw them, He said to them, "Go, show yourselves to the priests." And so it was that as they went, they were cleansed. And one of them, when he saw that he was healed, returned, and with a loud voice glorified God, and fell down on his face at His feet, giving Him thanks. And he was a Samaritan.

So Jesus answered and said, "Were there not ten cleansed? But where are the nine? Were there not any found who returned to give glory to God except this foreigner?" And He said to him, "Arise, go your way. Your faith has made you well." (Luke 17:11–19)

What an incredible indictment: the only one of those healed of their leprosy who returned thanks to God for his healing was a foreigner whom most Jews would have regarded as unclean, even apart from his leprosy. What sadness must the Lord have experienced at this lack of response to such an obvious gift. Yet many of us take the same attitude of entitlement. We ask, as God has told us to do, and yet when we receive, we do so with the attitude that we actually deserve what we have received. Here is no sense of humility, just self-satisfied complacency. When we take God for granted in this way, our blessings decrease, with the result that we start to feel that God doesn't answer our prayers. Our religion becomes depressed and lifeless, all because we have forgotten about the need for thanksgiving.

In the years of my ministry, I have had many people ask me to pray for many needs; very few of them have asked to offer thanks when those needs have been met. What does that say about our self-centeredness? What are we taking for granted? God is not a vending machine that cranks out the blessings when we put in enough change, but a gracious Giver who often responds, if what we request is in our best interest, even when we ask unworthily. If He ever starts to give us what we ask for when it is not in our best interest, we may want to duck!

✦ *Penitence* ✦

Penitence is the result of clear seeing. If we see God well enough to adore Him for who He is, we should also have a good idea of how short of His glory we are and understand just how unworthy we are of His love. This kind of humble understanding and prayer flows from adoration, because it is only the knowledge of how glorious God is that allows us to understand where we fit into things. Let's be honest: even at our best we are self-satisfied, generally focused on anything but God, and continually follow our own desires rather than seeking to do His will. Yet the Lord of glory still calls us to Him.

Before God, I am a sinner, and must humbly admit that. It was that kind of realization that brought forth Isaiah's lament about his unclean lips. But witness too that Isaiah's statement did not go overboard the other direction; he did not call himself snail slime or camel dung. He did not fall into the egocentric exaggerated penitence that can be such a spiritual trap, and which some of us find so enjoyable. God made us in His image and likeness, He loves us enough to save us, and these are glorious things. We are the apple of His eye. But in comparison to Him, we have fallen far short of the glory He intended for us, and penitence acknowledges that reality.

Humility and penitence result in confession, which should be a part of our daily prayer routine. I may wear all kinds of masks before my family, friends, and co-workers, but before God in prayer I must lay aside all pretense, admitting what I am and what I have done, asking for forgiveness of my sins. At the end of the day I need to look over my actions and confess those that have pushed me away from God, admitting my self-will and throwing myself upon His mercy. Penitence should be as natural to us as breathing, being rooted in a clear, sane sense of who we are without exaggeration or evasion.

✦ *Petition* ✦

When we have adored God, thanked Him, and humbled ourselves before Him, then we are ready to ask of God, stating our needs and seeking His blessings and gifts as a matter of grace. This kind of prayer is known as petition. Petition is unfortunately the only kind of prayer many Christians know, since they have actually been taught the spirituality of entitlement. Yet we can never demand of God. He is the all-powerful source of life; in Him we live, move, and have our being. Our prayers are but the movements of the Holy Spirit within us. Petition grows out of the other kinds of prayer, not out of our right to anything. But if we recognize who God is and who we are, knowing that we have no right to ask, then we can act upon His promises to supply our needs according to His will. Our greatest need is for God Himself, and this is our basic petition. We need God more than we need things from God, and the desire for God is the basis for our growth in Him.

Our petitions should cover our spiritual and physical needs, placing every part of our life in God's hands. We must remember an important point: when Jesus said, "Ask and you shall receive," He did not mean "ask for whatever you want and you will get it." Prayers of petition involve asking the Father in Jesus' name for what we need; the Son then asks the Father that *His will* for us be done in each individual case. "Now this is the confidence that we have in Him, that if we ask anything according to His will, He hears us" (1 John 5:14). Every asking of God is ultimately that His will be done for us; God knows so much better than we do the consequences of getting what we want. Our prayers of asking are not a negotiation in which we try to get the best deal we can, but the offering of our needs for God to sort out in a manner that is best for us.

We should be asking for spiritual gifts and virtues as much as for anything earthly. Humility, patience, an increased spirit of prayer, or a greater fervor in loving others: these things should be a regular part of our asking. And to make certain that our prayers do not focus exclusively on ourselves, we should make certain that we also petition on behalf of others in what is called intercession.

Intercession is a form of petition that involves prayer for the needs of others rather than ourselves, perhaps even requesting that someone else should receive the blessing we want for ourselves.

That should exercise the old humility muscles. The problem is that most of us ask things for ourselves frequently, for our loved ones when they are sick or in trouble, and for others in the world much more rarely. But if prayer unites us to God, who is the source and sustainer of all life, the closer we come to Him the closer we come to the whole creation, and the more important our relationship with the entire creation becomes. This includes many souls whom we don't even know, but who are in need of prayer. And although we are offering our own personal prayers, we do so as a part of the Church, and in fact as part of the royal priesthood of the Church.

St. Peter reminds us that we are "a chosen generation, a royal priesthood, a holy nation" (1 Peter 2:9). St. John Chrysostom refers to this in commenting on a passage in 2 Corinthians: "So you too are made a king and priest and prophet in the laver [baptism]; . . . a priest in that you offer yourself to God and sacrifice your body, and are yourself being slain also." We act as priests, offering ourselves and the creation back to God in gratitude for His giving it to us, because only to man has God given the ability and the responsibility to pray. As we offer intercession for the entire creation and its needs, we share in the eternal heavenly priesthood of Jesus Christ, joining our intercessions with those He offers to His Father.

This does not mean we have to pray specifically for every need of every creature, such as a special blessing for lemurs in Madagascar (assuming there are lemurs there). But we can offer the entire creation to God, who knows it and its needs better than we do, and let Him sort it out. What is important is that our priesthood is exercised and intercession is made. Some of the faithful reach such a degree of grace as to be able to pray continuously for the entire world, but they do so only after overcoming the passions and sustaining purity of heart.

Sometimes petition and intercession are very close indeed. In Matthew's Gospel, a Canaanite woman whose daughter is possessed by a demon confronts Jesus. When asking Him for help, she says, "Have mercy on *me*, O Lord, Son of David! My daughter is severely demon-possessed" (Matthew 15:22, emphasis added). She does not ask that her daughter be healed, but that she herself be helped. When Jesus does not immediately respond to her request, she continues crying out, "Lord, help *me*." This is the cry of the caregiver who accepts the situation her daughter is in, but who knows that on her own strength she cannot endure, she cannot continue to help. Yet because of her faith and persistence, it is her daughter who is healed, while at the same time her burden is taken away.

Some writers would list another category of prayer and call it praise. I do not see how that really differs from adoration and thanksgiving, and I suspect this distinction is over-definitive.

As with the spiritual rule, there should be balance within the life of prayer; we don't want to spend all our time asking for things for ourselves, or even for others, at the expense of glorifying God. On the other hand, intercession for the needs of others is an important part of exercising our royal priesthood. Even when we offer the Divine Liturgy, which glorifies God above all things, we include prayers and intercessions for others as we offer it "on behalf of all and for all." There may be times of crisis or illness, for example, when most of what we pray is intercessory; that is fine as long as we return to the balanced norm when the crisis is past. Do not be obsessive about the balance in your prayers; just remember to give God His due when you are asking something for yourself. Understanding the different kinds of prayer is not intended as a chain to keep you from functioning, but as a guide to enable you to pray in a flexible and mature way.

Chapter 5

Confession

There are two things about sin we definitely know. First, it is as inevitable as death and taxes: "If we say that we have no sin, we deceive ourselves, and the truth is not in us" (1 John 1:8). Sin is a reality for fallen human beings, and there is no way out of that. The fact is that we are tempted, fall, get up, are tempted, and then fall again. Any serious Christian knows there is a great gap between what we know we should do and what we actually do, so we can understand what St. Paul means when he writes, "I find then a law, that evil is present with me, the one who wills to do good" (Romans 7:21). There are times when sin seems to be an automatic, programmed response to temptation. Of course, no one makes us sin, but by its presence in our lives, sin is a sober reality we must all confront.

That brings us to the second thing about sin we should know: it can be forgiven. "If we confess our sins, He is faithful and just to forgive us *our* sins and to cleanse us from all unrighteousness" (1 John 1:9). Continuing, the writer expresses the hope that his readers will not sin, but if they do, "we have an Advocate with the Father, Jesus Christ the righteous. And He Himself is the propitiation for our sins, and not for ours only but also for the whole world" (1 John 2:1–2). We do not face sin alone, and we do not have to overcome it alone; we have God's grace and help in our fight against temptation. One of the weapons available to us is the sacrament of confession, sometimes also called penance, although those terms really identify separate parts of the mystery. It is a bad news–good news thing: when we sin, we need to go to confession; but when we sin, we get to go to confession.

In the sacrament of confession, we offer sincere repentance for our sins in the presence of our father confessor, and he then declares to us the remission of those sins according to Christ's promise. When Jesus appeared to His disciples in the upper room, following His Resurrection from the dead, He gave the Holy Spirit to them specifically for the ministry of forgiveness. "Jesus said to them again, 'Peace to you! As the Father has sent Me, I also send you.' And when He had said this, He breathed on *them*, and said to them, 'Receive the Holy Spirit. If you forgive the sins of any, they are forgiven them; if you retain the *sins* of any, they are retained'" (John 20:21–23).

Since the first days of the Church, the forgiveness of sin has been part of its purpose. This responsibility lay originally with the disciples and then was passed on to those they set apart to govern the churches they established—the bishops. In the apostolic and subapostolic ages, it was the bishop who led the worship and performed the sacraments, assisted by the deacons. The presbyters (priests) acted primarily as a council of advice to the bishop. But as time went on and each church became much too large for one man to pastor, presbyters were delegated to serve the liturgy and administer the sacraments in individual congregations. In more and more cases, this meant they were reconciling people to communion through confession of their sins. It took some centuries for the kind of system that exists now to evolve, in which people normally go to their parish priest for confession and reconciliation. But the idea that people should confess their sins in order that they might be forgiven and reconciled to the Church has been part of Christian practice since apostolic times. Only the method has varied depending on time and place.

❧ *The Purpose of Confession* ❧

The purpose of confession is to restore the purity of baptism, and in spiritual writings confession is discussed in baptismal terms. For example, St. John Climacus writes in *The Ladder of Divine Ascent* that "repentance is the renewal of baptism." In Step Five, he expands on this:

> Greater than baptism itself is the fountain of tears after baptism, even though it is somewhat audacious to say so. For baptism is the washing away of evils that were in us before, but sins committed after baptism are washed away by tears. As baptism is received in infancy, we have all defiled it, but we cleanse it anew with tears. And if God in His love for mankind had not given us tears, those being saved would be few indeed and hard to find.

The tears he refers to are those shed when we think of our sins and confess them, seeking to regain our purity.

When we are baptized, we die and rise to new life in Jesus Christ, and our sins are forgiven. We are as pure as Adam was before the Fall. Unfortunately, the reality of sin is that it is still there in the creation; it still confronts us and drags us down by temptation and our own weakness. We fall back, our souls become darkened and unable to perceive God, and we are cut off from our living bond with the Lord God. By being relieved of the burden of our sins in confession, we can be restored to life spiritually, strengthening our Christian will so that we can follow God once more.

When we go to confession, we state aloud, in the presence of our confessor, the sins we have committed that cut us off from God and from others. Always think in terms of the vertical and the horizontal when confronting your sins. Sin breaks communion between God and us: that is the vertical relationship; and sin breaks communion between others and ourselves: that is the horizontal relationship.

Certainly sin cuts us off from God: "Whoever abides in Him does not sin. Whoever sins has neither seen Him nor known Him" (1 John 3:6). There are plenty of sins we commit against God alone: despair, blasphemy, lack of faith, and so on. These break our communion with God. But there are many other sins we commit against each other, which break the unity in Christ we are all supposed to share. We never sin in a vacuum, and we are always sinning against someone.

We confess our sins in order to repent of them. Repentance does not just mean acknowledging our sins, because we could acknowledge them but not regret them; neither does it mean just being sorry for our sins, because we could be very sorry about everything and still not want to change. Truly repenting of sin means having the desire and the will to change the way we live and what we do. It means being willing to stop doing things that are wrong and replace them with doing right. It is important to understand this, because unless we realize that repentance involves change, it will have no effect in our lives. It is not enough to get rid of a vice; you must replace it with a positive virtue. In other words, you need to be willing to stop sinning. (You knew it would be something hard, didn't you?)

This means we must be willing to fight against our sinful inclinations with desire and a firm resolve, which, when united to God's grace, makes it possible for our souls to be healed and our lives to change. So often we confess our sins with a kind of hopelessness, a sense that we are just going to go out and commit the same sins again, so what is the use? And that is quite true if we have no desire to overcome our sinfulness. The spiritual struggle is a long and difficult way along which we are going to fall and fail many, many times. We need to recognize that, not with hopelessness, but with the same attitude that an athlete takes into competition. You know that you probably will not win each time you compete, but you enter the contest intent upon winning if possible, doing the best you can all the time. Combining your best effort with the grace and mercy of God can take you a long way down the road to perfection, even if you do not win each and every time, because you learn from each failure and apply what you have learned to the next part of the struggle.

Confessing your sins in the presence of your confessor is important for two reasons. It is humbling to admit your faults to another, and this works against the source of so many of our sins, our pride. We always want others to think the best of us, and it can be quite humiliating to repeat to someone who has heard them before the list of sins that seem to overwhelm us. This is good, because it forces us to acknowledge that we really are struggling, that we are not doing nearly as well as we would like to think, and that we have a long way to go. It also helps with that hopelessness that can settle in when we do not seem to be making much progress, the feeling that we may as well just give it up as an impossible job and stop torturing ourselves with thoughts of improving.

An experienced confessor can bring us to correction of the sins we have committed, remind us of times things have gone well, and point out the way to go when we can no longer see our direction clearly. As in spiritual direction, two heads are better than one; it helps to share the struggle. You can do that with other Christians as well; for the life of me, I don't know why our struggle with gluttony or pride should not be just as much a topic for conversation over a decent beer as the prospects of our team in the Super Bowl. But your spiritual father is the one to whom you can safely open the deepest problems of your soul. He has heard it all before, has carried the burden himself, and is appointed by the Church to declare God's forgiveness. Just getting the sin out before him is an important step in overcoming it.

✦ *Preparing for Confession* ✦

You should prepare for confession in the same way you prepare for any sacrament: by praying and fasting, and by asking God to allow you to see yourself clearly so you can uncover what needs to be uncovered. Do not worry if you are not aware of everything that is darkening your life; confession is a process that gradually takes us deeper into our soul, so that we become aware of the underlying problems that trigger our sinful responses. Any sin that has become habitual is called a passion in the Orthodox Tradition, and it can take a lot of confession of individual sins before we discover the underlying passions that control our souls.

Don't worry if you forget something that should be mentioned at confession; if you have made a sincere and faithful attempt to recall your sins, it will be all right. And remember that there are no sins that cannot be forgiven. All the remorse, anxiety, and guilt we load upon ourselves are unnecessary, because God is in the forgiveness business. We should not presume on that, and we must sincerely desire to be forgiven, rather than just getting through the distasteful task of acknowledging our sins; but if we desire to be forgiven, God is merciful and *will* forgive.

The word "contrition" refers to the sorrow or remorse we feel over our sins. In Latin *contritio* means to wear away something hard. The effect sin has on us, even when we are sincere in our relationship with God, is to harden our hearts to God's mercy until we feel no sorrow for what we have done. When we confess regularly, we wear away at the hardness of our souls, making it possible for us both to want and to feel God's mercy and love. This is why Jesus came to us: "For I did not come to call the righteous, but sinners, to repentance" (Matthew 9:13). God has taken the first step toward us. Confession means we take the next step toward Him.

Sometimes we worry that we might have committed an unforgivable sin. There are in fact references in the Bible to occasions when sin may not be forgiven, but in each case, the problem is from our end of things, not God's. For example, in Matthew's Gospel there is mention of blasphemy against the Holy Spirit, which "will not be forgiven men. Anyone who speaks a word against the Son of Man, it will be forgiven him; but whoever speaks against the Holy Spirit, it will not be forgiven him, either in this age or in the *age* to come" (Matthew 12:31–32). This is heavy stuff, but think on this: If someone blasphemes against the Holy Spirit, he is not open to receive forgiveness by the operation of that Holy Spirit. If he repents, that is a different issue. As St. John Chrysostom says in his commentary on this passage, "For even this guilt will be remitted to those who repent. Many of those who spewed forth blasphemies against the Spirit have subsequently come to believe, and everything was remitted against them." It is always a question of our willingness to repent, not of God's ability or willingness to forgive.

Sometimes the question is asked, "Why do I need to go to a priest for confession for my sins to be forgiven? Won't God forgive me if I just ask Him to?" The answer to this is "Yes." Remember that one of the kinds of prayer is penitence, in which we ask God to forgive the sins we have committed. If you stand in your prayer corner and ask God to forgive you for the sins you have committed that day, and do so with sincerity and genuine repentance, I have no doubt that you are forgiven. But that is not the only issue involved here. If you cannot get to confession regularly, confessing to God may be what you do much of the time. But we cannot forget that God has given the power to remit sins to His Church, and that means something; the struggle against sin doesn't take place in a vacuum, but as part of our life in the Church.

Think of sin as disease. If you are feeling sick, you could probably describe your symptoms to yourself and prescribe a course of treatment, but the chances of recovery are going to be less than if you went to a doctor. An experienced father confessor is one who can diagnose spiritual illness. When you are afflicted with it, you may not be objective enough to really understand what is happening. In the midst of your own pain, you may fail to see how to find a cure. You stand a better chance of getting well if you open up to your confessor, especially if he has been at this for a while. He can see patterns in the symptoms you describe, and since the Orthodox Church has been dealing with sin for two thousand years, if he is knowledgeable in the Tradition he may pinpoint your illness and lead you to a cure.

In addition, we have an obligation to the rest of the Church to function to the highest level of efficiency we can. That may sound odd at first, but remember that we are part of a living organism called the Body of Christ, that is, the Orthodox Church. Christian living does not take place in isolation, as St. Paul reminds us: "For as the body is one and has many members, but all the members of that one body, being many, are one body, so also *is* Christ. For by one Spirit we were all baptized into one body—whether Jews or Greeks, whether slaves or free—and have all been made to drink into one Spirit" (1 Corinthians 12:12–13).

He then goes on to speak of the various members of the Body of Christ and how each one must function properly for the Body to be whole. "But God composed the body, having given greater honor to that *part* which lacks it, that there should be no schism in the body, but that the members should have the same care for one another. And if one member suffers, all the members suffer with it; or if one member is honored, all the members rejoice with it. Now you are the body of Christ, and members individually" (1 Corinthians 12:24–27). If we are struggling against the passions and that struggle does not go well, it affects the other members of the Body.

Think of it as belonging to a sports team that depends on each member of the team playing up to his or her potential. You develop an injury or illness that makes it hard for you to play the way you should, yet you tell no one about this and seek no medical attention. You keep trying to overcome things on your own, hoping the situation will improve, which undercuts the efforts of your fellow players. It is a selfish, egocentric approach that breaks trust with the rest of the team. Trying to overcome sin without recourse to confession is like trying to cut down an oak tree with a nail file, refusing to use the chainsaw that God has provided. It makes the job much harder than it needs to be.

✦ *Penance* ✦

After hearing your confession, the priest may give you a penance to perform. A penance (in Greek, *epitimia*) is an action you do in offering to God, as a sign of your repentance and sorrow and sometimes to help you overcome one of the passions you are striving against. It may be something quite simple, such as a certain number of prostrations or prayers, a special fast, or perhaps even abstaining from receiving Holy Communion for a period of time. It is important to realize that this is not like paying a traffic fine and having your record expunged. The penance should not be seen as a legalistic penalty, but as part of the treatment for spiritual disease, to help and correct the penitent on the road to salvation.

St. Nicodemus the Hagiorite described the purpose of a penance in this way:

> The whole aim both to God and to the spiritual father is simply this, to bring about the return of the straying sheep, the sinner, to cure the one who has been wounded or hurt by the figurative serpent commonly called the devil, and neither to drive him to despair by heavy penances, nor again to let him take the bit in his teeth, like a horse, by light penances, and hence encourage him to contemptuousness and unconcern, but in every possible way, whether with austere or with mild remedies, to endeavor to restore the sinner to health and free him from the wounds of sin, so that he may taste the fruits of repentance, and with wisdom managing to help him ascend to the splendor of the Holy Trinity above.

The penance, then, is not something designed to satisfy a wrathful God who needs to get His pound of flesh from us. Neither is a penance always given, although it is certainly recommended in the Tradition; it may be that the confessor, persuaded of the sincerity of your repentance, will see no need for a penance. This does not mean your confession is a dismal failure, so do not go away disheartened. Trust your spiritual father's judgment in this. In fact, the confessor may not say anything except the absolution prayer. Confession is not therapy or counseling; sometimes the confessor may take the opportunity of your presence to say something in response, but again, the emphasis in confession is on your repentance and acknowledgment of sin, being humble before God, rather than on self-improvement. In-depth discussion of spiritual issues may be best conducted in the pastor's office when there is time to concentrate on the issues involved.

✦ Confession and Communion ✦

How often you should have recourse to confession is something that should be worked out between you and your spiritual father. If I am asked how often a person should confess, I will usually suggest every four to six weeks, especially if you are just getting used to making your confession. But it really depends on your own needs, and I do not think a rigid timetable is advisable, especially since it may need to change. Ask your spiritual father and follow his instruction. Never make changes in your spiritual discipline without speaking to and receiving a blessing from your spiritual father.

Remember, too, that there is a connection between confession and communion. In the twenty-eight years I have been an Orthodox priest, there has been a sea change in the way people prepare for Holy Communion. When I was ordained, it was not unusual for many Orthodox to receive the Eucharist only rarely, being held back by a sense of unworthiness. The ideal was that preparation for communion involved a long period of fasting—greater or lesser depending on which national group of Orthodox you were affiliated with—followed by confession. In recent years, there has been a much greater emphasis on frequent reception of the Eucharist as necessary for a healthy spiritual life, and this I agree with.

However, at the risk of sounding grumpy, it does seem that as the frequency of receiving Holy Communion has increased among Orthodox Christians, the sense of a need for good preparation has decreased. Many who receive Communion frequently do so without any regular confession. In fact, there are parishes where confession is not really taught as part of the preparation at all, and where fasting involves only abstinence from certain kinds of food. This must be discussed with your spiritual father. It is not necessary to make your confession before each Communion, but if we are frequent communicants, regular confession is also a necessity, along with fasting. The Body and Blood of the Lord should not be given out as a snack, but as the spiritual food we take so that we may have life. Our discipline should not get in the way of reception, but it must be a serious part of our preparation.

Remember to prepare for your confession with prayer, fasting, and reflection. Ask God to allow you insight and humility. Many good guides to confession are now in print, such as the one contained in the little red prayer book published by the Antiochian Archdiocese. If you need to write down some notes to help your memory, that is fine, and if you do forget something, do not worry. In Orthodox worship we refer to the fact that God is good and loves mankind. Like the father in the parable of the Prodigal Son, if we move towards Him, He will run to meet us, sweeping us into His loving embrace.

Chapter 6

Asceticism I: Exterior Disciplines

B y exterior discipline I mean here those external acts of self-discipline by which we try to overcome the passions, purify our hearts, and train our bodies. This discipline is absolutely essential for Christian living and is rooted in the teaching of the New Testament. In the first chapter we read what St. Paul had to say about the necessity of such training. In Colossians he makes the point again: "For you died, and your life is hidden with Christ in God. When Christ who is our life appears, then you also will appear with Him in glory. Therefore put to death your members which are on the earth: fornication, uncleanness, passion, evil desire, and covetousness, which is idolatry. Because of these things the wrath of God is coming upon the sons of disobedience" (Colossians 3:3–6).

"Put to death your members which are on the earth": those are strong words, but they indicate how hard a struggle we face when we try to overcome sin and grow in love. Orthodox Christian life is meant to be an exercise in love rather than constant penance; but penance and the spiritual discipline that expresses it will always be necessary for us to grow in Christ. Remember that we are "heirs of God and joint heirs with Christ, if indeed we suffer with Him, *that we may also be glorified together*" (Romans

8:17, emphasis added). Asceticism is part of the way we join in Christ's suffering in order to share in His glory.

❧ The Need for Discipline ❧

And this is the point at which some people will have a first-class, full-blown, flat-out gut reaction against the whole idea that there is a physical side to spirituality. Some will see this as a masochism rooted in the Dark Ages and practiced to an unhealthy degree by ignorant monks, which should be avoided by the sane. Others, with their eyes firmly fixed upon the inessential, will start salivating at the prospect of long vigils in the middle of the night, three-hundred–knot prayer ropes, and bodies emaciated by rigorous fasting. Neither response is appropriate. Spiritual discipline is not an end in itself, but only a means to an end, which is growth in faith and love. It should neither be undervalued nor overly prized, but should simply form part of that balanced spirituality that helps us cope in our relationship with God, others, and the whole of creation. As Abba Moses, one of the Desert Fathers, wrote, "Therefore fastings, vigils, meditation on the Scriptures, self-denial, and the abnegation of all possessions are not perfection, but aids to perfection: because the end of that science does not lie in these, but by means of these we arrive at the end."

Ascetic discipline is firmly laid down by our Lord in the Gospels, as we shall see, and is a firm part of the Tradition. St. Thalassios wrote, "The forceful practice of self-control and love, patience and stillness, will destroy the passions hidden within us." Learning to focus on what is important and avoiding distraction is the purpose of asceticism, and it is required if we are to suc-ceed in anything we want to do well. Whether you are a doctor, a lawyer, a teacher, or anything else, you must learn discipline if you are going to increase in knowledge and expertise. How much more is this true in spiritual things. If we are going to serve God, we cannot serve ourselves, and the way to serving Him is through prayer and ascetic discipline.

One of the reasons we often reject the idea of asceticism is that we just do not like to be disciplined. Few people I know like to exercise, yet exercise of some kind is necessary for a sound mind and body; without it we become lazy and unhealthy. I climb on my bicycle and try to ride about nine or more miles a day. I hate the thought of doing it, but I also know that the benefit in terms of my blood pressure and general well-being is immense. What is true of our bodies is also true of our souls. When it comes to spiritual health, many of us are ninety-pound weaklings, the kind who have Satan kicking sand in our faces all the time.

This is especially true of those who look at spirituality as a child does at a candy store. They see it in terms of a sweet, sentimental mysticism, expressing Christianity without the Cross, without any real sacrifice. These are people who have "a zeal for God, but not according to knowledge" (Romans 10:2). It is positively scary how many people want a kind of instant spiritual high without doing any work. In our instant-gratification society, many Orthodox can fall into that trap.

It is possible to quote the Fathers and not have the faintest idea of what is taught in the Scriptures, or to have an unhealthy interest in liturgical rubrics but not know how to make a good confession. Religious externals can be a snare for the unwary that diverts attention from things like humility and repentance. If you find yourself more familiar with the writings of St. Gregory of Sinai than with St. Matthew's Gospel, or if you would rather read about prayer than pray, you have a problem that concentrates upon the dessert before the solid food. That undisciplined approach to religion produces no fruit in a life, since it remains on a superficial level. As with everything in the spiritual life, you need adequate guidance for what you try to do: it is as important to speak with your spiritual father about fasting and other bodily austerities as it is about prayer and confession. Anything self-taught is problematic, because we tend to be either too easy or too hard on ourselves—although in the beginning, trying to do too much seems to be the greater problem.

✦ Fasting ✦

Fasting is an ascetic discipline mandated and practiced by our Lord, who began His public ministry with a forty-day fast. "Then Jesus was led up by the Spirit into the wilderness to be tempted by the devil. And when he had fasted forty days and forty nights, afterward He was hungry" (Matthew 4:1–2). Well, duh. Of course He was hungry, but that was not the point. His fasting was a challenge to Satan—He deliberately went into the wilderness to be tempted—the start of a very public spiritual war that would reach its climax on the Cross. He threw down the gauntlet to the devil and had to deal with the consequences, all of which you can read about in Matthew 4. This is an important point: Fasting is not just an exercise in discipline, although it is that. It is a rejection of the devil's temptation to turn stones into bread, or to put it in a wider context, to use the creation as a means of feeding ourselves, to consume it as a thing in itself without any reference to God. It was, after all, an act of eating that led to trouble in the first place.

Adam and Eve had been placed in a paradise of plenty, which is called in the Bible Eden: "The Lord God planted a garden eastward in Eden, and there He put the man whom He had formed. And out of the ground the Lord God made every tree grow that is pleasant to the sight and good for food. The tree of life was also in the midst of the garden, and the tree of the knowledge of good and evil" (Genesis 2:8–9). Later He tells Adam, "Of every tree of the garden You may freely eat; but of the tree of the knowledge of good and evil you shall not eat, for in the day that you eat of it you shall surely die" (Genesis 2:16). So Adam is turned loose in the Farmer's Market with a free pass to the produce, with just one exception: he could not eat of the fruit of one tree. He had to follow one rule, and he couldn't do it! It must have driven him nuts. Imagine him walking up and down, muttering about that one tree. Why was that so important? It was like putting someone in a quiet room free of distraction and saying, "Now, you may think about anything you want, but whatever you do, do not think of a three-armed gold monkey." You are going to have gold monkey on the brain.

So when the serpent tempts Adam and Eve, they fall for it and break communion with God. The Bible account can be interpreted on many levels, but it comes down to this: by an act of disobedient eating, mankind broke the intimate relationship that had existed between God and His creation, and this results in spiritual death. This is the death that God had prophesied for Adam. God did not kill Adam—the wound was self-inflicted; but through it all the disease, chaos, and death we associate with human life were let loose on the world.

So it should hardly be surprising that the second Adam, Jesus Christ, put a priority on fasting; it reverses Adam's disobedience. This is not the whole of His teaching, but it does at least begin at the beginning. What is good for Jesus is good for His adopted brothers and sisters, all those who have been joined in baptism to Him. So He says, "Moreover, when you fast, do not be like the hypocrites, with a sad countenance. For they disfigure their faces that they may appear to men to be fasting. Assuredly, I say to you, they have their reward. But you, when you fast, anoint your head and wash your face, so that you do not appear to men to be fasting, but to your Father who is in the secret place; and your Father who sees in secret will reward you openly" (Matthew 6:16–18). Jesus says, "when you fast," not "if you fast." Our participation in this practice is assumed, as a means of sanctification for all.

Fasting is important not just for the sake of obedience but for other reasons as well. It cuts our dependence on food, drink, and the other material things that tend to get in the way of our relationship with God. Eating is a natural, normal thing that is necessary to sustain life, but as with many positive virtues, we often turn it into a vice by indulgence in various forms of gluttony. Gluttony is not just the sin of overeating; it is the sin of overdependence and misuse. We use food and drink to cover our insecurities and to avoid problems, feeding ourselves for pleasure and security rather than for need. As a result, we become trapped in a life of self-indulgence that itself is a twisted kind of self-affirmation—we give ourselves the approval we don't feel we are getting from others in the form of food. This is a misuse of the creation and an abuse of ourselves.

Fasting is the self-discipline that helps liberate our bodies and souls from this kind of false comfort. In addition, fasting helps to sharpen the senses, so that prayer and reflection become more focused on God rather than ourselves. If we are going to be more attached to God, we must be less attached to material things, not because material things are bad—everything God created is good—but because we oftentimes wind up being more in love with material comfort than we are with God. By fasting and other forms of detachment from material things, we are trying to give our whole self to God, so that all our will and love and hope can be in Him. Avoiding pleasure for its own sake, even that available on PBS, we find pleasure in God.

As with any spiritual discipline, there are pitfalls to be avoided, and Jesus Himself refers to them. He warns against practicing our piety before others, so He lays down some rules for the kind of fasting He wants His followers to do. Specifically, we are told to avoid doing anything that would draw attention to the fact that we are fasting. He sure knows how to take the fun out of it. In a sermon given on fasting, St. Augustine of Hippo writes, "For in this work also we must be on our guard, lest there should creep in a certain ostentation and hankering after the praise of man, which would make the heart double, and not allow it to be pure and single for apprehending God." If our fasting is mixed with a certain secret desire for people to notice us, we really are not concentrating on God, and our fasting will not be for the purification of our souls. This means that when you fast, you should not express irritation about fasting or what you are or are not allowed to eat, or ask others what they are doing, or come into church for Lenten services staggering as if faint from hunger. All of that just feeds the ego, and the devil blesses the effort.

But there is more to Jesus' teaching than the negative fact of avoiding recognition for our spiritual effort. It is worse than that; we are supposed to be happy! Jesus speaks of anointing the head, and washing the face, and acting as if this entire exercise in self-discipline were somehow enjoyable. So it should be—if we are seeking the Kingdom of heaven. The joy of soul and purity of heart that result from proper fasting should be our delight; the liberation from having the flesh control us, rather than the other way round, should lead to a real sense of triumph. Contrary to popular myth, the Christian religion is not meant to be one long exercise in pain and depression, but one of freedom in Christ. Overcoming the passions and gaining godly control over our lives should be a matter for rejoicing!

Fasting is not an end in itself. During Lenten periods, Orthodox Christians often seem to border on the obsessive about fasting, but little else. Fasting is only one tool among many. The universal teaching of the holy fathers is that prayer and fasting are linked: if you are not praying, do not try to fast, because you will fail. Your fasting will be an external act of discipline that merely becomes a burdensome complaint. During periods of greater effort, such as Great Lent, if you do not increase your praying, I suspect you should not increase your fasting. Really, it may do you more harm than good by increasing your physical burden without any interior lifting of the heart, which leads to bitterness and complaint. Fasting alone will do little to help us transform our lives. St. Nicetas Stethatos taught, "Judicious fasting and vigils, together with meditation and prayer, quickly lead to the threshold of dispassion." But that, he wrote, is true *provided* the soul possesses humility, is full of the tears of repentance, and has a love for God. It is ascetical discipline made up of many different kinds of effort that tames our soul and leads us to purity of heart.

Prayer is part of this effort as well: prayer in vigil, which is a period of time in which we are watchful against intruding thoughts (not necessarily at night); meditation, when we prayerfully reflect on the Scriptures or writing of the saints; use of a prayer rope if we have been given that discipline; the physical act of prostration during prayer—these are only part of what should be linked with our fasting to keep the entire self subdued and maintain our focus on God.

And although this is probably getting old, I have to say again, do your fasting under the guidance of your spiritual father. People have different levels of strength when it comes to fasting; those who are older, or ill, or very young cannot fast at the same level as those who are young and healthy. The rules the Orthodox Church sets down during fasting seasons should not be seen with legalistic eyes; they are goals we strive for—external guides meant to facilitate inner change.

✦ *Almsgiving* ✦

Almsgiving is another form of spiritual discipline meant to aid detachment from material things. "Therefore, when you do a charitable deed, do not sound a trumpet before you as the hypocrites do in the synagogues and in the streets, that they may have glory from men. Assuredly, I say to you, they have their reward. But when you do a charitable deed, do not let your left hand know what your right hand is doing, that your charitable deed may be in secret; and your Father who sees in secret will Himself reward you openly" (Matthew 6:2–4). Once again, Jesus gives quite specific instructions that seem to be primarily aimed at the humility-challenged. The Lord reminds us that external actions such as giving alms are intended to bring about an inner transformation rather than to garner worldly praise.

Almsgiving is charitable giving for those in need; it is not the same thing as the pledge or tithe that you give to support your local parish, even if a portion of that may be designated by your church to help those in need. Alms are the monetary gifts you give for the aid of others over and above other giving. Jesus warns against doing this in public because He knows how easy it is for our pride to get wrapped up in our good works. The danger is that we can get used to being praised for what we are supposed to be doing as a matter of course, and when someone forgets to pat us on the back we suffer a letdown. All of this pushes both our pride and our self-affirmation buttons, and suddenly we are dealing with another passion or two.

St. John Chrysostom says this kind of giving should be done "with complete modesty: secret, noiseless giving." This doesn't mean that you should feel bad about doing good, or sneak around in the dead of night to slip your check under the church door, but that you should always be concerned about motivation if you want to make progress in dealing with your passions. St. John of the Ladder warns that we must always be on the lookout for the frog in the bucket, referring to the fact that sometimes when water is drawn from a well, a frog comes along for the ride. Any virtue can turn into a passion: hospitality can turn into gluttony; anger against sin can turn into anger against your brother, and so on. The demons are on duty 24/7 looking for ways to twist up your spiritual life, which is why we must be vigilant and watchful. It is all right if someone knows you are giving alms, or if they tell you that it is a good thing to do; you just need to leave it at that. "But this is what is blamed in them," St. Augustine of Hippo writes, "that they act in such a way as to *seek* the praise of men . . . For the question under discussion is the cleansing of the heart, which, unless it be simple, will not be clean."

None of our ascetical actions, be it fasting, prayer, almsgiving, or anything else, is an end in itself, but all are intended to cleanse our hearts by liberating us from the passions. When I give alms, I take from what is mine, from what I would like to keep in my pocket or bank account, and give it so that someone else can benefit from it. I learn to get by on less so that someone else can get by with something. I could put the money in the bank and earn interest off it to my benefit, but if I did that while someone else went hungry, I would be condemned. If I give, I will have a little less money to invest, and I may have to depend on God a bit more than I do now, but I will have taken the focus off my needs and put it on someone else's. This helps liberate me from avarice—the need to accumulate material goods. However, if I sought praise for my giving, I might overcome avarice only to be overcome by pride—hence the caution about not being praised by men.

✦ Detachment from Worldly Things ✦

Detachment from worldly things may even require abandoning certain relationships as part of our spiritual discipline. One of the harder things that Jesus says in the Gospels is, "He who loves father or mother more than Me is not worthy of Me. And he who loves son or daughter more than Me is not worthy of Me. And he who does not take his cross and follow after Me is not worthy of Me" (Matthew 10:37–38). It would be a disturbing thing to be judged unworthy of Christ, and yet He sets up such an extreme demand that we might wonder if anyone can really follow Him in the way He demands that we should.

There is nothing wrong with caring about our families and friends: Jesus never says we should stop loving anyone. In fact, He says we should love our neighbors as ourselves, but all other loves must take second place to our love for God, because if we elevate earthly relationships to first place we have become idolaters. What we often think of as love for another is in fact simply a physical, emotional, or spiritual desire for another that we have not kept within proper bounds by making our love for God central. It is also possible that the love we feel for another, if love for God is not predominant, will lead to temptations we cannot withstand; this can be particularly true in sexual relationships, which can start out as friendship but end up as something else. If our relationship with another person has become an emotional idolatry, then we may need to leave that relationship behind if we are to continue walking with God. It is not just bad things that get in the way of being with God, but good things to which we have too great an attachment.

We need to exercise custody over our senses, by which I mean we need to be careful what we look at and listen to. It is through the senses that external images enter the mind to distract and tempt us. What do we read or watch on television and in the movies that leads us, if not simply to distraction, then to fantasy and concentration on ourselves? It need not be something erotic; much of our daydreaming just wastes time that could be profitably used for study and prayer.

Cultivate silence as much as you can by keeping radio and television usage within sane boundaries. Most people talk far more than they need to, so set a watch over your mouth. Do not seek opportunities for conversation when there is no real need. We should be listening for God, which can be hard if He cannot get a word in edgewise. Keeping silent prevents us from saying stupid or sinful things we will regret later. "Even so the tongue is a little member and boasts great things. See how great a forest a little fire kindles! And the tongue *is* a fire" (James 3:5–6). Or, as Abraham Lincoln said, "It is better to remain silent and be thought a fool than to speak and remove all doubt."

Always remember that we follow ascetical acts and disciplines only so that we may seek closer union with God. Never examine your own actions in a spirit of competition with others, and never judge the actions of others in light of your own. Seek the advice of your spiritual father in this as in all else. Each person has his or her own strength level, and some may be able to handle stronger discipline than others; this doesn't make them better or even closer to God, but it does mean that they must be willing to work up to the level of their own strength. God blesses all effort if it is made in sincerity and love.

Chapter 7

Asceticism II: Interior Detachment

The last chapter dealt with the external, visible actions that are meant to detach us from worldly distractions. This is the first step towards living in inner freedom. The second step comes through interior detachment, the purpose of which is to purify our hearts so that we may unite our spiritual powers and join them to the will of God.

⇀ *Purity of Heart* ↼

Inner detachment is about purifying the heart so that we can freely communicate with God, learning His will for us so we may accomplish it. What do we mean by purity of heart? Jesus taught, "Blessed *are* the pure in heart, for they shall see God" (Matthew 5:8). He also taught, "Where your treasure is, there your heart will be also" (Matthew 6:21). Abbot Moses, who was one of a group of early ascetics known as the Desert Fathers, taught his monks that the ultimate goal of Christian life was the Kingdom of God, but the "immediate aim or goal is purity of heart, without which no one can gain that end." This is true for everyone, not just monastics. Unless we clear out those things that darken our ability to perceive God, the distractions and attachments that keep us from focusing, our journey to the Kingdom will be difficult at best.

But purifying the heart is not just a matter of avoiding the entanglements that get in the way; it is a matter of loving with a single focused love. St. John Cassian writes, "Perfection is not arrived at simply by self-denial, and the giving up of all our goods, and the casting away of honors, unless there is that charity which consists in purity of heart alone." The heart is mentioned a great deal in Orthodox spiritual writing, and it refers to that reasoning, intelligent part of the soul that is called in Greek the *nous* and is seen as the center of the spiritual life.

Charity is that love that the Holy Spirit has implanted within our hearts. This is not an earthly love, the kind of enlightened self-interest that passes for love with so many of us, but a love that has its source in God: "the love of God has been poured out in our hearts by the Holy Spirit who was given to us" (Romans 5:5). When we receive the Holy Spirit at baptism, God's love comes with it as part of the package, and this love is very single and focused; it is one.

We tend to think of purity as something negative, the avoidance of any kind of defilement, but it should be thought of as something positive. Purity does not simply mean avoiding things that are impure, or a freedom from all desires for other things; it carries the sense of something complete with nothing alien mixed in. Pure gold is all gold, with nothing else added. I have a jar of honey in the pantry that says it is pure white honey; that means there is nothing else added to it.

Purity of heart therefore means singleness of purpose and desire. A person who is pure of heart has no other desires except the desire for God. One of the Desert Fathers said, "The palm tree has a single heart, which is white, containing all that is good. One meets the same thing amongst the righteous: their heart is simple, seeing only God; it is white, having the illumination that proceeds from faith; and all the work of the righteous is in their hearts." The heart is where we have our deepest desire, or our treasure, as Jesus taught us; so our hearts must be single and simple, undivided by sin.

But how can we achieve this? Most people's hearts are a mess of contradictions and confusions, and we are often unaware of what desires are driving us. How then can we focus on our desire for God? We are so entangled in the desires of this fallen world that trying to cut ourselves clear of them can seem absolutely overwhelming. How can we avoid the distraction of so many voices calling to us? Is it even possible to become pure of heart? Yes, if we have the desire for it, if we are willing to work persistently, patiently, and with humility.

✦ *Controlling Our Thoughts* ✦

The first thing we need to do is seek to control our thoughts. What could be easier? The Holy Fathers label as intrusive thoughts those images, fantasies, and concepts that disjoint our thinking and seek to capture the intelligent, reasoning part of our soul. Such thoughts may start off as simple suggestions that we can turn aside without too much effort, while other thoughts may be passion-charged memories of past sins linked with images of sinful actions that catch us up in replaying past sins. St. Maximus the Confessor writes that a memory such as that of a person or an object (such as gold) presents itself as a simple thought, while a passion is a "mindless affection or indiscriminate hatred for one of these same things." In other words, the thought of something and our obsession with it join together, making a combination of passion and image. We must strive, he writes, to separate the passions from the image.

We strive to keep our thought simple by being vigilant and exercising self-control. See—it's easy! The thoughts themselves may come from our memory, or they may come from outside by some external stimulus; that could mean from the devil, but it could just as easily be the *National Enquirer*. St. Thalassios wrote that thoughts could come from our senses, memory, or our own temperament. If we tend to be, let's say, choleric by nature, we may find it quite easy to merge anger with the thoughts that wander by.

We need to distinguish between evil thoughts and the good thoughts that come from God. Your own response to the thought can help you here—if a thought suggests joy, that thought is from God, but if a thought leads to a darkening in your heart, that may be a good sign that its source is not God. St. Barsanuphios taught, "When a thought suggests to you to act according to the will of God, and you find in this matter joy, and at the same time a sorrow which fights against it, know this thought is from God. . . . The thoughts that come from the devil are filled with disturbance and dejection, and they draw one after them secretly and subtly." Always test the spirits, for it is possible for thoughts rooted in pride and self-indulgence to induce joy. If you have trouble figuring out just what your response should be, such as when you see your mother-in-law drive over a cliff in your new Mercedes, check with your spiritual father!

The basic cause of evil intrusive thoughts is our own fallen state and the spiritual warfare that we find ourselves in the midst of. The demons are always trying to capture our hearts with sinful thoughts so that they will lead to sinful actions, keeping our attention upon ourselves so that we focus on the care and feeding of our desires; they seek to make us self-indulgent. St. Maximos writes, "The passions lying hidden in the soul provide the demons with the means of arousing impassioned thoughts in us." In other words, the devil uses the passions that exist in our soul to launch attacks at our most vulnerable points. This is why Jesus teaches us, "But those things which proceed out of the mouth come from the heart, and they defile a man. For out of the heart proceed evil thoughts, murders, adulteries, fornications, thefts, false witness, blasphemies" (Matthew 15:18–19).

This does not mean that we produce evil thoughts naturally, but they come about because we remember past sins, especially if they were pleasurable, and particularly if we are not open in confessing our sins or sharing our thoughts with our spiritual father. When we hold things back, we keep them in our heart and give the demons ammunition for their attacks. What is worse, we often hold onto evil thoughts for the sheer pleasure of remembering the things we have done or the things that have been done to us; so in addition to sinful pleasure, anger, or resentment, we have set ourselves up for an attack. This is especially true when we are not actively trying to repel the thoughts or distractions that bombard us. We have little control over what comes at us from without, and the mere fact that a thought or image pops up is not in itself sinful. But we so often ask it in for a cup of coffee and discussion, which gives it a chance to settle into our soul, and then we are hooked and provoked to sinful actions. For this we have only ourselves to blame.

How can we deal with intrusive thoughts? By paying attention to what we are thinking instead of being mindless about it, by cultivating silence, and by rejecting the intrusive thoughts when they do come. We know, or at least should know, that temptation is out there and that we need to be careful about it. "Be sober, be vigilant; because your adversary the devil walks about like a roaring lion, seeking whom he may devour" (1 Peter 5:8). In a fallen world we have to deal with sin and the thoughts that try to provoke us to action. It's not difficult to know when thought encounters brain; we need only pay attention to the thoughts that come in order to decide whether a given thought must be resisted. Yet often we don't pay attention. We let all kinds of thoughts and images rattle around in our heads on the assumption that a little thought never hurt anybody.

✦ *Cultivating Stillness* ✦

An essential tool in the struggle is silence or stillness, which we need to develop in order to think clearly. The Greek word for this is *hesychia*, which refers to a watchful silence. If we are to guard our mind from thoughts, as well as our soul from passions, we need to be able to control what is going on with our thoughts and emotions in order to examine them. Hesychia doesn't mean just being disconnected from outward stimulations, but being still and calm in our hearts. Becoming agitated or excited about intrusive thoughts is not a good way to deal with them, because the agitation itself can lead to sinful action. Genuine spiritual struggle is patient and persistent. This is an atmosphere we can cultivate first within us, and then around us. It does require controlling outside stimulation, and that means seeking places that are quiet where we can focus. Trying to deal with your interior life while watching CNN is not going to work; therefore, we must cultivate a detachment from worldly distractions.

Another line of defense against intrusive thoughts is simply to reject them, to cut them off before they can ensnare us. We cannot control what comes at us from the outside, since we are constantly bombarded by the images and thoughts that exist in the world around us. In modern culture there almost seems to be a conspiracy to prevent us from being alone with our own hearts, what with televisions playing in airports and advertising coming in over our cell phones. Much of this, while deliberate, is not aimed specifically at us as individuals, but is meant to get a response from certain classes of people: the young, soccer moms, older white males, or what not. It is the white noise in the background of our lives that prevents us from concentrating on anything except the messages that others wish us to hear. This is a greater problem now than at any other time in history because of advances in the technology of communication. If St. Antony went to the desert because he felt there was too much distraction in the city of Alexandria in the fourth century, imagine how he would react now, with billboards, newspapers, and film at eleven.

So we are stuck with a lot that comes at us, and even if we are watchful and silent, some intrusive thoughts will get through. "Just as it is impossible to stop a watermill from turning, and grinding both wheat and tares, the mind is in constant motion," St. John Cassian writes. We cannot just stop thoughts, so when the spiritual writers say to cut them off, they mean to stop them by an act of will before they make it into our souls. As mentioned before, do not invite the thought in for coffee and conversation, trying to understand why it is there or where it comes from—break the connection with it. Stand up to it: mocking the thought can be helpful, ridiculing it before it gives any of the satisfaction that would lead us to sinful action.

Rebuke the demons that are active in this, letting them know that you are aware of what they are trying to do and you are not falling for it. (St. Isaac states, "Our sense cannot come to know evil or be incited by it without the mediation of the demons.") Pointing out that the demon is ugly and its mother dresses it funny, or that it is stuck in a dead-end job or will never get a date with a decent woman—in other words, mockery—is another powerful weapon. Make fun of it and chase it out of there—the demons cannot stand being mocked. But be careful! Make certain you are not attempting feats of strength that are above your spiritual pay grade. We are all at different levels of maturity, and taking on a bully before you are ready could turn into a real disaster.

If you lack confidence in your ability to make a frontal assault, it may just be safer to resort to fervent prayer instead of getting in evil's face. St. Maximos warns those who don't feel confident in this warfare, "Those who still fear the war against the passions and dread the assaults of invisible enemies . . . must keep silent; in their struggle for virtue they must not enter into disputes with their enemies but through prayer must entrust all anxiety about themselves to God." St. Gregory of Sinai wrote, "When thoughts come, call to our Lord Jesus, often and patiently, and they will retreat; for they cannot bear the warmth of heart produced by prayer, and they flee as if scorched by fire." Use the Jesus Prayer, or the short form, "Lord, have mercy," as a means of blocking intrusive thoughts and rebuking the demons involved with them (they don't like prayer). Concentrate on the words rather than the thought. In this way we join the heart and the mind together, struggling on both levels. Be persistent and faithful, and you will prevail over the distracting thoughts. Do not expect it to be either quick or easy.

Confess your thoughts to your spiritual father so that they do not stay in your heart as fertile ground for temptation. St. John Cassian reminds us, "He who conceals his thoughts remains unhealed." This helps us get a handle on our anger and desires. Ask for your spiritual father's prayers, as well as those of others, so that you can overcome the thoughts. I do not mean just a quick "Please pray for me," but a specific request for his intercession for specific issues. Avoid situations that are a temptation to you, but avoid people who are a temptation as well. Get some exercise, read the Scriptures and the lives of the saints. When we begin to be freed of control by our thoughts and emotions, we have really begun to walk the path that leads to God's Kingdom.

Chapter 8

The Passions

Passions. There, I wrote it. Of course you read sex, or at least something sensual, because in our culture that tends to be what we connect with the word "passion"—it isn't as if we're obsessed or anything. Yet most common definitions of the word refer to suffering and emotion, as well as love: being driven to act by outside forces, or being ruled by our emotions. This is what the word actually means.

When used in Scripture it tends to have the emotion connotation, rather than referring to sexual things. For example, in Galatians 5:24 St. Paul writes, "And those *who are* Christ's have crucified the flesh with its passions and desires." In this verse, "desires" is the "s" (sex) word. In Colossians 3:5, St. Paul is even more explicit in separating passions and sexual acts: "Therefore put to death your members which are on the earth: fornication, uncleanness, passion, evil desire, and covetousness, which is idolatry." This does not mean that our emotions are not connected to our sexuality—they certainly are—but that the passions deal with other issues in our personality as well. In these passages, passion is closely connected with the disorderly forces of human nature that must submit to the rule of the Holy Spirit. (To "put to death" means to bring to an end the unchecked activity of the passions; in other words, to gain control over them.)

✢ Passion and the Fall ✢

To understand the passions and how they work, we need to speak a bit about sin. More specifically, we must think about humanity's Fall. We are all familiar with the story of what happened in the Garden of Eden—perhaps too familiar, because we get wrapped up in snakes, fruit, and guilt without a deeper understanding of the Fall's cosmic dimensions. When God created us, He gave to us three indispensable gifts: freedom, reason, and love. All three are necessary for our spiritual growth and blessedness, but all three also have a downside. For example, most people would say they want to be free with no one controlling them, so that they can make their own choices in life. Indeed, freedom without choice is an oxymoron: being locked into a behavior pattern in which we can choose only to do that which is good is not freedom but slavery. For there to be genuine freedom, there must be the possibility of choices between right and wrong; or to put it another way, there must be the possibility of temptation.

The temptation for our faculty of reason is pride, becoming proud in our mind, which means that rather than acknowledging that God is the source of wisdom and goodness, we seek the knowledge of good and evil outside of God. This is what God forbade Adam and Eve to do when He told them not to eat of the fruit of the tree in the midst of the garden. When they ate of that tree and came to know the source of good and evil, they were striving, in effect, to become God.

The temptation for love is to turn it away from God and others and to aim it at ourselves, so that we become self-loving and egocentric. Instead of finding our happiness in God, we look for it in ourselves and in all the material things that satisfy our desires and give us temporary enjoyment.

Adam was created as an infinite potential, with the opportunity to grow towards or away from God. These temptations were placed before him, and he caved. Adam's Fall was not an accident or the result of bungling, but the result of a deliberate choice. Genesis makes it clear that Adam and Eve were led to temptation, but the decisions were theirs.

> Now the serpent was more cunning than any beast of the field which the LORD God had made. And he said to the woman, "Has God indeed said, 'You shall not eat of every tree of the garden'?"
>
> And the woman said to the serpent, "We may eat the fruit of the trees of the garden; but of the fruit of the tree which is in the midst of the garden, God has said, 'You shall not eat it, nor shall you touch it, lest you die.'"
>
> Then the serpent said to the woman, "You will not surely die. For God knows that in the day you eat of it your eyes will be opened, and you will be like God, knowing good and evil."
>
> So when the woman saw that the tree was good for food, that it was pleasant to the eyes, and a tree desirable to make one wise, she took of its fruit and ate. She also gave to her husband with her, and he ate. (Genesis 3:1–6)

Subtle the devil may have been, but he had no power to force Adam and Eve to respond to his suggestions. (The Orthodox Tradition has always interpreted the serpent to be Satan.) However, other than the carb problem, what was the big deal about eating the fruit? The sin was in this: when they accepted the devil's temptation, they violated the direct command of God, failing to trust Him to know what was best for them. Had they rejected the temptation, they would have shown both obedience and trust in God, which are the bedrock foundation for a relationship with Him. By exhibiting humility and self-control, they would have begun the process of deification. In commenting upon the Fall, St. Augustine of Hippo wrote:

> Here is pride, because man desired to be more under his own authority than under God's; and a mockery of what is holy, because he did not believe God; and murder, because he subjected himself to death; and spiritual adultery, because the immaculateness of the human soul was defiled through the persuasion of the serpent; and theft, because they made use of the forbidden tree; and the love of acquisition, because he desired more than was necessary to satisfy himself.

Wow: all that for a piece of fruit.

The results of this for us are the poisoning of our moral life, which makes any return to holiness impossible for us on our own; the loss of the immortality of the body, which makes the immortality of our soul a curse and subjects it to judgment; and the loss of Paradise, of our life in the Kingdom of God. We are deprived of the future blessedness of which Adam and Eve had a foretaste in Paradise. Instead of eternal life, we are subject to death, darkness, and rejection by God. The only thing that can rescue us from this is the coming of the Redeemer: "For I know *that* my Redeemer lives, / And He shall stand at last on the earth; / And after my skin is destroyed, this I know, / That in my flesh I shall see God" (Job 19:25–26).

All of this is what we call original or ancestral sin: the contagion (not the guilt) we inherited from Adam that drives us to hopelessness and more sin. Because actions have consequences, the result of ancestral sin is that we have cut ourselves off from God in our soul and have a tendency to sin. We have not been deprived of our natural power to choose good, but our souls have been darkened; we are not as responsive to God as we were meant to be, and our sinful tendencies have become a disease from which we cannot heal ourselves. This leads us into the passions.

❖ *What Are the Passions?* ❖

The English word "passion" is linked to the Greek word *pascho*, which means "to suffer." Certainly the passions cause suffering, to ourselves and others, and trying to overcome them definitely leads to suffering as we try to reshape our lives according to the image of God. The fact is that serial root canals might be preferable to dealing with some of our favorite passions.

Essentially, a passion is any sin that has become habitual for us, whatever that sin may be. For some people, the passions may indeed be sexual in nature, especially if we are addicted to controlling and manipulating others into meeting our sexual desires, using sex as a way of exercising power. But for others the passions may be other things: lying, gossip, greediness—the list is almost endless. Basically, a passion is a sin that has become so ingrained in our nature that it is really a sickness that dominates and drives our life. Indeed, this can go on so long and become so ingrained that Orthodox spiritual tradition would make a distinction between the passion and the sin, even though they were at one time the same. The passion becomes the interior action of the soul that is expressed outwardly in sinful acts by the body. And although we have to struggle against outside influences such as intrusive thoughts, a passion can become so much a part of us that it really needs no external spark, but can live long and prosper in the realm of fantasy.

Jesus speaks of the inner origin of the passions when He teaches the disciples the source of what really defiles us. "And He said, 'What comes out of a man, that defiles a man. For from within, out of the heart of men, proceed evil thoughts, adulteries, fornications, murders, thefts, covetousness, wickedness, deceit, lewdness, an evil eye, blasphemy, pride, foolishness. All these evil things come from within and defile a man'" (Mark 7:20–23). Now Jesus here is speaking specifically to the issue some people had with eating unclean foods, but then He gives it a much wider application. Why obsess about eating the wrong foods when all these other problems can get their hooks into us?

We have seen that outside temptations can be fought against and need not get a response from us, but with the passions we need no outside stimulus. Thus we need to look to reshaping our inner man in order to grow more like Christ. The passions are not coming from outside us, but from within, as an interior response to temptation; we have met the enemy, and he is us.

Generally, the Orthodox Tradition sees the passions as a corruption of the natural powers of the soul that have been distorted by sin. As long as we live in isolation from God, this corruption of natural powers darkens our lives. "For when we were in the flesh," St. Paul writes, "the sinful passions which were aroused by the law were at work in our members to bear fruit to death" (Romans 7:5). The only thing that can change this state is to orient ourselves to God and allow the Holy Spirit to work in our lives. St. Paul goes on, "But now we have been delivered from the law, having died to what we were held by, so that we should serve in the newness of the Spirit and not *in* the oldness of the letter" (Romans 7:6).

St. John of the Ladder writes, "Evil or passion is not something naturally implanted in things. God is not the creator of passions." In his book, *The Ladder of Divine Ascent*, in which he recounts the various levels of spiritual growth, St. John continues, "On the other hand, there are many natural virtues that come to us from Him. We have taken natural attributes of our own, and turned them into passions." For example, sex turns into fornication, anger against evil becomes anger against persons, and our natural need for food turns into gluttony.

In other words, the lives we have now, which we regard as being natural and normal, are not so. Sin has messed with this, breaking the communion that existed between God and His creation and turning everything on its head. Ancestral sin has darkened our vision of the world. The way we use other people and the world for our own ends and purposes is the result of darkened and corrupted powers that had their origin in God, but are now twisted into something else. Eating is not evil, but it gets twisted into gluttony; sex is not evil, but we use it selfishly and only for our own pleasure; speech is a godly gift, but we use it to gossip and slander. Natural is good, as God says in Genesis each time He creates anything, but our sins have taken the creation and twisted it in ways that would make Gumby scream. From the world's perspective, being controlled by the passions is just the way you get along; from God's perspective, the passions must be overcome as we are transformed from darkness into light.

The greatest passion of all, the one that leads to everything else, is self-love, which causes us to turn from God and concentrate upon ourselves excessively. Somehow it is always about us, even when we are doing something good. This distortion can come about more easily than you might think, because we have a wonderful plan for our life. If we are absolutely convinced that our way is the correct way in all circumstances, whether we actually say that or not, we have been nailed by self-love. All are afflicted by sin, so even the best of us, the holiest of us fall short and are capable of getting wrapped up in ourselves. Getting things right again doesn't mean beating ourselves up, but reorienting ourselves toward God. While that is easier said than done, we have been given the tools to do the job: repentance, humility, obedience, prayer, and confession.

✦ *The Genesis of the Passions* ✦

Passions may originate in the intrusive thoughts discussed in the last chapter; the link is so strong that it can be hard to understand whether a writer is referring to struggling against a thought or against a passion. The connection between thought, sin, and passion is not a simple one. Certainly, if the thought precedes the passion, the link between the thought and the passion is what must be broken if the passion is to be overcome. But just so you don't think this is easy: It is possible that a thought may lead to sin, which may become a passion; but it is also possible that an existing passion may give rise to a sinful thought and then a sinful action. If we commit this sin often enough, it may become a passion, which then may give rise to corresponding evil thoughts.

Assuming that we are dealing with the path from thought to passion, the process goes something like this: A thought may enter the soul, where it gets our attention and holds out the prospect of pleasure. What kind of thought is not really important; it could be a desire for your next-door neighbor or a desire for a Sam Adams lager, because it is the pleasure principle that provides the bait. This is just a temptation at this point, not a sin; but the anticipation of the pleasure is the bait that gets our attention. We need to cut it off at this point, because if we do not, we begin a dialogue with the pleasure that provides the hook. We give our assent and are reeled in. The increasing prospect of pleasure captures our soul and weakens our resistance, and so the sin is committed, either outwardly or inwardly. When the capture is repeated, we have a passion.

Fantasy plays a large role in this process, because fantasy increases the prospect of pleasure, and this leads to easier consent—and God knows we are easy enough to begin with. This is why the saints wrote so much about self-control. It is also important to remember that the passions have no essence of their own, but as St. John of the Ladder reminds us, are natural powers that have been corrupted by our withdrawal from God. God does not create the passions in order to yank our chain.

There are passions that afflict the body and passions that afflict the soul. The following is meant as an introduction that will not cause your eyes to glaze over, but mentioning some of the passions may give you an idea of what to be watching out for. St. John of Damascus lists some of the bodily passions: gluttony, greed, drunkenness, secret eating (ouch), stealing, self-adornment, using cosmetics (take that, Mary Kay!), wasting time, daydreaming (remember the role fantasy plays in sin), sexual sins, sacrilege, consulting oracles, casting spells. He lists some passions of the soul as well: impiety, heresy, blasphemy, anger, backbiting, boastfulness, forgetfulness, laziness, indecision, dejection, irritability, fear, jealousy, envy, pride, grumbling, ingratitude, and love of popularity. He and other writers list many more, but I don't want you to maintain that fetal position any longer than necessary.

All of these can interact with one another, can be found in various combinations, and may depend on our state in life. For example, St. John of the Ladder says that for those who live in the world, avarice would be the greatest temptation, but for monks it would be gluttony; given the monastic emphasis on fasting, that would certainly make sense. Some of the common combinations are anger and lust, gluttony and lust, and self-esteem and laziness ("I am too important to work").

It is possible for a virtue to be turned into a vice if we are not watchful of what we do. Hospitality can turn into gluttony as we keep all that food from going to waste; love can certainly turn into unchastity; and discernment can become cunning. This is why, as we said before, St. John of the Ladder says to watch out for the frog in the bucket. Any time we try to live by the flesh—that is to say, on the world's terms—rather than according to the Holy

Spirit, we are asking the passions if they can come out to play. "I say then: Walk in the Spirit, and you shall not fulfill the lust of the flesh. For the flesh lusts against the Spirit, and the Spirit against the flesh" (Galatians 5:16–17).

It is not enough to avoid the passions; it is not enough to push them down. The passions must be transformed; otherwise they just wait there for us to drop our guard so they can rear up and bite us. Just as virtue can turn into vice for the unwary, it is necessary to replace vice with virtue if we are to succeed in overcoming the passions. This is what it means when we read in the Bible:

> Therefore put to death your members which are on the earth: fornication, uncleanness, passion, evil desire, and covetousness, which is idolatry. Because of these things the wrath of God is coming upon the sons of disobedience, in which you yourselves once walked when you lived in them. But now you yourselves are to put off all these: anger, wrath, malice, blasphemy, filthy language out of your mouth. Do not lie to one another, since you have put off the old man with his deeds, and have put on the new man who is renewed in knowledge according to the image of Him who created him (Colossians 3:5–10).

The Orthodox Tradition understands putting to death as transformation, since even physical death, for the Christian, results not in the destruction of the body but a transforming of it, as Christ's body was transformed after the Resurrection. We must be renewed in knowledge after the image of our Creator.

Chapter 9

Go Towards the Light

As Orthodox Christians we are meant to grow and to be transformed; it is all part of becoming a new person in Christ. "But we all, with unveiled face, beholding as in a mirror the glory of the Lord, are being transformed into the same image from glory to glory" (2 Corinthians 3:18). Our salvation is a process of transformation from living our lives according to earthly principles—according to the flesh, as Scripture often puts it—to living according to spiritual principles, or, in Bible-speak, walking in the Spirit (refer to Galatians 5:16). Unfortunately, although we had unveiled faces (souls) after baptism, the reality of sin darkens our vision, making it harder to respond to God because we cannot communicate clearly with Him. It is like what happens to your vision when cataracts start interfering with your eyes; clear sight must be restored if life is ever to return to what it should be. The passions must be transformed.

✦ *We Cannot Do It Alone* ✦

The passions are transformed by the joint action of God and ourselves. We cannot do it alone, because our own effort, however well-meant and focused, will not be enough. Me, myself, and I, even with the help, support, and cheerleading of others, cannot transform darkness into light. The reason is a simple one—there is only one source of light, and that is Christ.

St. Makarios of Egypt once preached a sermon that would have done credit to Billy Graham, who would have understood perfectly what he meant; he said that we cannot "be saved without Jesus, or enter the kingdom of heaven." Any plan of salvation that does not include encountering Christ is fatally flawed. There is only one source of light, and that is Christ: "Awake, you who sleep, / Arise from the dead, / And Christ will give you light" (Ephesians 5:14). Only by cooperating with the Giver of light will we be able to cease associating with the darkness and walk in light.

Now many of you who profess yourselves Christians may be thinking, "This is basic stuff. Why be so obvious? We paid good money for this?" But the fact is that we tend to ignore the obvious, engaging in the fine art of dodging repentance by concentrating on ourselves. Remember that the greatest passion is self-love. Even when we understand that, even when we realize it is not supposed to be always about us, we still try to overcome the passions by our own effort, with only *pro forma* references to God. We will pray, of course, fast, confess, do all the things we are told to do, but because we keep thinking in terms of *our* effort rather than God's grace, we do not make much progress and probably go in for a great deal of grumbling.

For example, we may have a whopping big list of sins we rattle off at confession, and yet wonder why we don't feel any better for it, as if just listing them were important. Did you really think God did not know what your sins are? The purpose of confession is to be responsible, humble, and accountable for what you have done, not to inform God of what He does not know. If you just listed your sins to fill up God's time without any sense of having failed Him, without being fully accountable (with no blame-shifting) for what you have done, without listening (with no argument, interior or otherwise) to whatever your confessor says—then you are trying to transform the passions on your own, and you will fail. You can be ensnared by the passions even when trying to do good.

So we start with a profound acknowledgement of divine grace and our need for it, not just formally, but really. We are saved by this grace, and it is God's wonderful gift given to us by the Holy Spirit; but then we must cooperate with it, for this is the way we change. It would be equally wrong-minded to think that our passions will be transformed by God alone; He could do that, certainly, but then we would have contributed and learned nothing, exercising no obedience, humility, or love. If we live in the Holy Trinity, we have the tools, but we must learn to use them. In Orthodox Tradition, we call this "synergy": this means we work together with God to produce the changes that are necessary in our lives as we offer our faith and life to Him. Our healing is accomplished by Christ's divine energy, which is available to us because we have been joined to Him in baptism. Only if we are in Christ and with Christ can we "walk in the Spirit" (Galatians 5:16), that is to say, live in the grace of the Holy Trinity. Our job is to work as hard as we can to reject the control of the passions so that God can transform them.

* Opening Ourselves to Grace *

We open ourselves to God's grace by loving Him and seeking Him as the greatest love of our life. It is not enough to say, "I love God"; we must *be in love* with Him as well. Anyone who has ever cared about another person knows there is a profound difference between saying you love someone and really being in love with that person. When you are in love with someone, your entire world revolves around the one you love, you want to be with him or her all the time, and—here it comes—*you must care more about that person than about yourself*, if your love is a genuine love. If you don't care more about the other than about yourself, you are in like, not in love. This is the problem for so many—they like God, but they really don't love Him in the way He deserves to be loved, in the way we need to love in order to change. Until you can love God more than yourself, you will never change.

Next you need to repent, which requires a certain amount of insight. You have to know that you are a sinner, and believe it or not, there are even Christians who have a problem understanding that. I have had people come to confession with nothing to say beyond reading the prayer in the book. When I asked them if they had anything to confess, they said, "No," and quite honestly meant it. They felt that since they had not murdered any in-laws or had an affair with the person next door, they were home free. This is not how it works. St. Paul reminds us that "all have sinned and fall short of the glory of God" (Romans 3:23), and in 1 John we read, "If we say that we have no sin, we deceive ourselves, and the truth is not in us" (1 John 1:8). We are sinners; we are fallen. There is no way to avoid that, because we have been born into a world that has been warped by sin, and we have been shaped by it. We may not be Charles Manson, or even Benny the Dip, but we sin in all kinds of ways, small and great.

The English word "sin" translates the Greek word *amartia,* meaning to fall short or miss your aim. Where I come from, gun control means being able to hit what you aim at, so we understand that anything off the mark by God's standards is sin. Not only do you not win the turkey; you may go to hell if your aim doesn't improve. That towel you took from the Holiday Inn was actually stolen, and you need to repent of the theft. Remember when your great aunt called, and you told your child to inform her you weren't at home when you really were? Ditto.

This is important, because we may have passions in need of transformation that we are not aware of because we are not acting out on them, or at least we think we aren't. That "borrowing" of a Holiday Inn towel might be the first act that leads to the passion of avarice, or it might be the outward manifestation of a passion that has been hidden for years until being aroused by the kitsch fashion of a motel bathroom. St. John of the Ladder wrote, "Watch out continually for signs of the passions and you will discover that there are many within you." The towel is a minor thing, but the passion of avarice is not.

We must be willing to look into ourselves and to do so clearly, seeing with God's eyes what our passions may be. Take, for example, those little quirks we keep making excuses for, like that continuous sense of irritation we carry with us through the world, or our habit of always inflating our successes. These are indications of deeper sickness within us. So we seek to know who we really are and repent, which means to take responsibility for our actions rather than blaming someone else. "Well, Father, I do drink too much, but if you really knew what my wife was like, you would understand why." Perhaps your wife is the way she is because you drink, but that isn't the point either. No one forces us to sin, so be responsible for what you have done; confess your sins and no one else's.

The most readily available source of grace is in the sacraments and worship of the Church. In these, God pours His energy into our lives, if we receive them in a reverent and prepared manner. There are sacraments such as baptism, chrismation, confession, and communion that all must share in, and there are others, such as marriage or ordination, that are limited to those specifically called to those states—all are true wells of living water. The Holy Eucharist is the crown of them all, in which God gives Himself as the nourishment that sustains and strengthens our lives. Likewise with worship, that ever-flowing river of grace that washes over and around us when we come together to be the Body of Christ.

Confession has already been mentioned, but it needs to be emphasized. We will never overcome the passions without frequent, honest confession to a competent confessor who will not be fooled by our "spin." Just offering confession to God in prayer, without anyone else present, leaves us unaccountable to the rest of the Body of Christ and allows us to cut ourselves too much slack; it is simply one more way of dodging repentance. If you had children who had misbehaved and you needed to know what they had done wrong, would you be satisfied with "I'll confess what I did to God," and let it go at that? Being truly accountable requires witnesses.

Additionally, if you have sinned in a major, soul-destroying way, don't wait until your next scheduled confession to deal with it. Don't defer confession of major sins, for they build up quickly and darken our soul, helping the passions to take root. Follow this simple rule: when in doubt, spill your guts. If you don't really need to be there, if you are being a bit too scrupulous for your own good, an experienced confessor will know and can tell you; but that should be his decision rather than yours. St. Thalassios wrote that subordination to a spiritual father coupled with self-control is what subdues the wild beasts of the passions. Lastly, Satan knows full well how valuable confession is to the soul, so he will throw up all kinds of reasons and objections why you should not confess regularly. So confess your sins often—it drives the devil nuts.

Cultivating simplicity of life and exercising control over our senses are two more ways in which we transform the passions, since many of the passions are connected to material things. It is so easy to get obsessed with the care and feeding of your lifestyle. Maintaining a simple life—such as keeping our bills to a level that we can pay, as well as other prudent financial management—removes one major area of stress that tests many Christian souls. God promises to meet our needs, rather than our wants, but we often do not understand the difference. We can become frustrated, irritable, and greedy when He does not turn out to be the cash cow that some Christian teachers today proclaim Him to be. We have to maintain control over our lifestyle if we are going to transform passions such as greed and avarice.

In the same way, exercising control over our senses—what we look at, what we listen to, what we taste and touch—is necessary to prevent some passions from taking root, and to transform those already rooted. Guarding our eyes against things they should not see is not the easiest task in our culture. It is hard to drive along a road without being assaulted by an over-the-top billboard, or to avoid seeing things on television during the "family hour" that make us blush; but we need to be diligent in this. Obscene and erotic speech or song lyrics flow over us like a running stream, and we become so used to them that they seem almost normal. But what we hear disturbs the soul, and as with the temptations of the eyes, helps feed the fantasizing that lead us into sin.

Even the senses of smell and taste can bring memories of old sins, or situations of sin, or just that wonderful gourmet meal at the very time when we should be fasting; these distract the heart from concentrating on God. It is a lot easier to prevent a passion from taking root than to transform it later; but even if it is rooted, it is easier to change it if we keep it from getting stronger. It would have made sense to take fasting seriously fifty pounds ago instead of trying to gain control over gluttony now, but it is still easier to do now than when they have to roll you out of the house to the hospital.

We transform passions by following the teachings of Christ, taking seriously the way He calls us to live. I am sometimes amazed at the number of men (and I suppose women now as well, because you have all come a long way, baby) who think it is all right to look at a member of the opposite sex in a sensual manner as long as you don't do anything about it; look, but do not touch. (Clean mind, clean body: take your pick!) Wrong. Jesus' teaching could not be clearer: "You have heard that it was said to those of old, *'You shall not commit adultery.'* But I say to you that whoever looks at a woman to lust for her has already committed adultery with her in his heart" (Matthew 5:27–28). He says something similar about anger.

As St. Gregory the Theologian said, "There is little difference between 'to hear' and 'to do'." It is not enough to be externally in control; in order to deal with the passions, you must be internally in control as well. Remember that the passions often live in the realm of fantasy. If we live a two-level existence, carefully controlling our outward behavior but running loose inside, we can give up any hope of truly purifying our souls and transforming our lives. The old law covered external behavior, but in Jesus' teaching the external rules of "Thou shalt not" become internalized. Our inner and outer lives must be in synergy as well; otherwise we simply become psychotic—spiritually if not mentally.

Purity of heart means being focused and sane, not playing games with our emotions and senses. Our heart is one because it does not have competing loves that it must keep sorting out, and our true love is Jesus. If that is fixed and firm, we can have love for many other people, sometimes very deep love; but we will not have other loves.

✦ *Transforming Negative to Positive* ✦

There is a negative and a positive aspect to transforming the passions, and they must be seen as two sides of a coin. This is why we speak of transforming instead of simply overcoming a passion. It is entirely possible to cut off a sin from your life, ending the bad habit so that you no longer participate in that particular sin, and still be caught up in the stress and tension that sin can produce in us. How can that be, when we have struggled so hard to overcome something bad in our souls? We wind up questioning whether it was really worth the effort. Certainly it was; any time you remove a poison from your soul, it is healing. But we may not reap the full benefit of the healing, because we have left a hole where the sin used to be; we have not replaced it with anything positive.

Jesus spoke of a man who removed a demon from his life only to have more demons take up residence. "When an unclean spirit goes out of a man, he goes through dry places, seeking rest; and finding none, he says, 'I will return to my house from which I came.' And when he comes, he finds it swept and put in order. Then he goes and takes with him seven other spirits more wicked than himself, and they enter and dwell there; and the last state of that man is worse than the first" (Luke 11:24–26). The demon was displaced and order made in the house, but because nothing positive had replaced him, there was still a place for demons to dwell. If all we do is remove something negative, rather than seeking to transform it into something positive, we leave a vacuum, which both nature and the demons abhor.

For example, if a man struggles to overcome an addiction to pornography, he may stop looking at sexually explicit pictures and get rid of the magazines and videos. He may, with great struggle, fasting, and prayer, block temptation out of his mind—for a while. But unless he begins to look at women in a positive manner, as human beings to be loved as God loves them rather than seen as sex objects; and unless he begins to see that sex is a God-given gift meant to express a deep and abiding love rather than to be used as a means of gratification, he is going to have other demons move in.

Pick your passion—unless you replace the negative with a positive, you will not be able to transform it. Paul once wrote about a man who was a thief; have him work with his hands, the apostle instructs, for the benefit of others. If he simply stops stealing, he is a thief who is temporarily unemployed. But if he concerns himself with supporting others, getting his focus off himself and his passion, he can transform the negative into a positive and probably overcome the passion. If you are into gardening, the idea of pulling up vice and planting virtue may resonate. The point is that transformation involves changing the nature of our passions, not just ejecting them. If we cannot do this, we simply hang ourselves out to dry.

What kind of virtues can be cultivated to replace the negatives? Humility is a major virtue, without which there is no Christian living worthy of the name. Such things are the fruit (or the result) of the Spirit working with our spirit, living and growing in the grace of God. Until we learn to value others and their ideas at least as much as ourselves, and recognize that we are not always right, we will always be fighting against self-love and pride.

In Scripture other virtues are also called the fruit of the Spirit: "But the fruit of the Spirit is love, joy, peace, longsuffering, kindness, goodness, faithfulness, gentleness, self-control. Against such there is no law" (Galatians 5:22–23). You can practice love by always seeking what is best for others rather than for yourself; you can transform gluttony with fasting, anger with patience, laziness with physical activity. Work at self-control so that your responses to people or situations do not lead to occasions for sin. Seek out good and holy things to occupy your mind and soul. "Finally, brethren, whatever things are true, whatever things *are* noble, whatever things *are* just, whatever things *are* pure, whatever things *are* lovely, whatever things *are* of good report, if *there is* any virtue and if *there is* anything praiseworthy—meditate on these things" (Philippians 4:8). Sometimes we can sink into the pit contemplating all the garbage that seems to overcome the world, allowing it to overcome our hearts. Part of our spiritual effort should be to seek out what is good in order to rejoice in it. For different folks there may be different things—for one Mozart and for another Johnny Cash; but whatever is good and beautiful is Orthodox, so rejoice in it.

Another way in which we may need to transform the passions is to accept, in a godly and patient manner, the pain they may cause in our lives. A soul that is struggling against the passions is an unruly soul, and God has several means to bring it under control; pain is one of them. If we can accept from the hand of God the adversities that can happen to us, we can transform the passions. The pain we may endure in this life can be one way of mortifying the passions and purifying the soul. Not everyone has to deal with pain; on the other hand, God never said that getting our ticket punched meant we would get out of this world unhurt. We may be spiritually unharmed, yes, but that is a different thing.

So pain and suffering, accepted with patience and joined to Christ's suffering, may be a means of purification and union. "I now rejoice in my sufferings for you, and fill up in my flesh what is lacking in the afflictions of Christ, for the sake of His body, which is the church" (Colossians 1:24). What could possibly be lacking in what Jesus suffered for His Church? My part in it, if that is what God's will for me is. Thus it is important that I understand that what I suffer in this world is for my transformation and salvation. God gives to the soul, which is darkened and weak, first forgiveness and then grace, so that it may be crucified in the flesh and have something to offer God in union with Christ.

Pain without any meaning is a truly frightening thing, but for Christians it has meaning. It is the means by which we can purify our souls and transform the passions, especially if we have been lax in ascetical effort. The fact is that the pain you have in your knees may very well be there because you have not knelt enough in prayer, because you have not purified yourself with fasting and self-control. To the world, which has been taught to avoid discomfort whenever possible, that seems mad; but it is the teaching of the saints.

A word of warning here: there are people with a lifetime membership in the Society for Creative Masochism who spend their lives looking for ways to hurt, enjoying pain with the enthusiasm worthy of a better cause. Do not become one of them. Trying to live a godly life in a fallen world will result in struggle and pain—either spiritual, emotional, or physical. It is not necessary to seek out pain. Doing so is not spiritual but sick. It will transform no passion, but will probably feed several.

It is best to deal with the passions one at a time rather than in one big lump. It can be intimidating to stand axe in hand before an entire forest, but if you take it one tree at a time, you can make some progress cutting them down. If you have a dominant passion that seems to overrule all the others, then tackle that one first, since it is unlikely that you will make any progress against the others until you have gone after the big one. That doesn't mean you can go ahead with other sins meanwhile, but you can focus your main effort on one while continuing a holding action against the others.

Pray fervently; do not become discouraged by the struggle; seek good direction and counsel. The passions did not appear overnight, and neither will their healing; but with perseverance and God's grace, we can purify our souls.

Chapter 10

Jerusalem, the Heavenly City

Spirituality is not an end in itself, but a journey on which we encounter God and enter the Kingdom of heaven. Any genuine Christian spirituality must be centered in God, leading us to encounter Him in our daily lives in much the same way that Moses encountered the Burning Bush, discovering a presence that would not be ignored. Moses did not head out to find God that day:

> Now Moses was tending the flock of Jethro his father-in-law, the priest of Midian. And he led the flock to the back of the desert, and came to Horeb, the mountain of God. And the Angel of the LORD appeared to him in a flame of fire from the midst of a bush. So he looked, and behold, the bush was burning with fire, but the bush *was* not consumed. Then Moses said, "I will now turn aside and see this great sight, why the bush does not burn." So when the LORD saw that he turned aside to look, God called to him from the midst of the bush and said, "Moses, Moses!" And he said, "Here I am" (Exodus 3:1–4).

Moses was going about his daily work, but he was open to investigating God's presence when he came up against it. What he found was more than an interesting sideshow. "Then He said, 'Do not draw near this place. Take your sandals off your feet, for the place where you stand *is* holy ground.' Moreover He said, 'I *am* the God of your father—the God of Abraham, the God of Isaac, and the God of Jacob.' And Moses hid his face, for he was afraid to look upon God" (Exodus 3:5–6).

Here is a real difference between genuine spirituality and what so often passes for it: genuine spirituality leads us to face God as He is. It is nice to play at spirituality, mixing in teachings from different religions, keeping things user-friendly and juggling interesting ideas, and it is a marvelous way to avoid dealing with God. As long as we can keep comparing differing traditions and swapping ideas, we need never really deal with the fact that God is a person, not an idea. But if we are going to be truly spiritual, we must face Him, and as Moses found, that can be a bit frightening.

Conversion begins when we face God, and Christian spirituality is about being converted. Only truly meeting God will let us see the great gap between what we are and what He has called us to be. Only this will push us down to our knees, flat on our face in contrition and joy. This is what spirituality is all about—conversion, change, and union with God: Father, Son, and Holy Spirit. Only God can give us the grace we need, and only we can cooperate with that grace. The spiritual life is our life of cooperation with God's grace so that we may be saved, so that we may dwell in His Kingdom, so that we may enter the New Jerusalem.

Sin means choosing self instead of God. Genuine spirituality means choosing God and accepting His call: "For I *am* the LORD your God. You shall therefore consecrate yourselves, and you shall be holy; for I *am* holy" (Leviticus 11:44). To be holy is to be separate, different and unique. God is completely different in His existence from anything we can imagine, and that is what He has called us to be, making that possible by allowing us to become "partakers of the divine nature" (2 Peter 1:4). As we become so, we begin to understand that loving God means giving Him absolutely everything, holding nothing back for ourselves.

In whatever state of life we are in, as monastic or married, clergy or laity, spirituality is the way we try to give it all to God. It is the way we learn to return love for love, since "we love Him because He first loved us" (1 John 4:19). As St. Benedict wrote in his *Rule*, "Through this love, all that he [the monk] once performed with dread, he will now begin to observe without effort, as though naturally, from habit, no longer out of fear of hell, but out of love for Christ, good habit and delight in virtue. All this the Lord will by the Holy Spirit graciously manifest in his workman now cleansed of vices and sins."

✦ *Living in the Kingdom* ✦

Genuine spirituality is about living in the Kingdom of God, something we can do because Jesus has brought the Kingdom to us: "Now after John was put in prison, Jesus came to Galilee, preaching the gospel of the kingdom of God, and saying, 'The time is fulfilled, and the kingdom of God is at hand. Repent, and believe in the gospel'" (Mark 1:14–15). Spiritual life is not about seeking some abstract ideal, some holiness that is unattainable and therefore quite safe; it is about living in the Kingdom of God, which is a present fact.

Living in the Kingdom is about the practical working out of our lives by God's grace, allowing it into every little nook and cranny, finding God in everything we do, no matter how small or unimportant it might seem. We will encounter God as surely in doing the dishes as in feeding the poor, for if we live in the Kingdom of God, all things are filled with Him and we see Him in all things. There is no division into what is sacred and what is not, because all our tasks are offered to and blessed by God.

The Kingdom is a gift from the Father that we can live in eternal life. Jesus taught His disciples, "Do not fear, little flock, for it is your Father's good pleasure to give you the kingdom. Sell what you have and give alms; provide yourselves money bags which do not grow old, a treasure in the heavens that does not fail, where no thief approaches nor moth destroys. For where your treasure is, there your heart will be also" (Luke 12:32–34). It is in the Kingdom of God that we discover what is most important to us. It is in the things we hold most dear in our hearts, most precious beyond any earthly treasure, that we find God's Kingdom. Our life of union with God the Holy Trinity is that unfailing treasure that cannot be taken away from us if we maintain our life in the Kingdom. It is about holy living and holy dying, and anything in between that we may have forgotten about. Genuine spirituality is about living ordinary life in an extraordinary way.

Jesus said that we must repent and believe because the Kingdom is at hand, and this we do in the Church, the Spirit-filled presence of the Kingdom of God. If we have been baptized and regularly receive the Holy Eucharist, then we are living in the Kingdom, finding life in Christ, who meets every need. "I am the bread of life," He said. "He who comes to Me shall never hunger, and he who believes in Me shall never thirst" (John 6:35). Here He refers not just to earthly needs, but to every spiritual and emotional longing and need we have. All will be satisfied by the divine energy given to us in the sacraments and worship of the Church. In the Kingdom of God, we find a foretaste of the glory and joy that will be ours in the Kingdom of heaven.

Heaven is our ultimate goal, the heavenly city, New Jerusalem. How often do you think of heaven? For a place in which we will spend eternity, it seems to occupy a very small place in the thought of many Christian people. How easy it is to allow spirituality to become a substitute for heaven, letting the journey become more important than the destination. The first taste of the Kingdom is already here if we are living truly spiritual lives, if we live in anticipation of the coming of the fullness of the Kingdom with power and great glory.

Christians believe that history will have an end and that the Lord will return. "For the Son of Man will come in the glory of His Father with His angels, and then He will reward each according to his works" (Matthew 16:27). The purpose of spirituality is to prepare us for the end, when "the Son of Man comes in His glory, and all the holy angels with Him, then He will sit on the throne of His glory" (Matthew 25:31). Jesus has been given authority by the Father to judge the world, and spirituality shapes us in holiness so that we can be among those who are told, "Come, you blessed of My Father, inherit the kingdom prepared for you from the foundation of the world" (Matthew 25:34). After the world is judged, then God will be all in all.

In Revelation 21, the New Jerusalem is depicted descending to earth so that the dwelling of God will be with men. This is our inheritance.

Now I saw a new heaven and a new earth, for the first heaven and the first earth had passed away. Also there was no more sea. Then I, John, saw the holy city, New Jerusalem, coming down out of heaven from God, prepared as a bride adorned for her husband. And I heard a loud voice from heaven saying, "Behold, the tabernacle of God is with men, and He will dwell with them, and they shall be His people. God Himself will be with them and be their God. And God will wipe away every tear from their eyes; there shall be no more death, nor sorrow, nor crying. There shall be no more pain, for the former things have passed away. (Revelation 21:1–4)

The separation that came about between God and His creation as the result of Adam's Fall will be no more. We will no longer be on the wrong side of a great divide between God and man. The creation will not be as it was in the beginning, but as it was meant to become, with God in the midst of us. What a glorious life this will be, in a purified, restored creation in which there is no past or future, only "now" with God. The word "eternal" does not imply time without end, but having no sense of time at all. We will not be aware of how long we are with God, only that we are. There is no temple in this city, nor formal worship services (that may be a relief for some of you), for what need will there be for a temple when we are physically in the presence of God? All sorrow, sickness, disease, and need will have been banished. "He who overcomes shall inherit all things, and I will be his God and he shall be My son" (Revelation 21:7).

Toward the end of the description of this great and heavenly city, the point is made that the gates of the city will never be shut; there will be nothing to prevent people from entering the city. And yet some people will stay outside of their own will. Some will not enter because they have been sidetracked by false teaching and slick spirituality; instead of seeking Christ they hold discussions about Him.

Orthodox spirituality is about purifying our souls so that we may know God's will and do it, and be loved into holiness by God. Only in this way can we enter the gates of the city which shall never be shut by day, and where there is no night. May you find your way to the heavenly city.

Other Books of Interest

❧ *Also by Fr. Michael Keiser* ❧

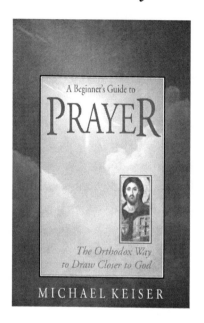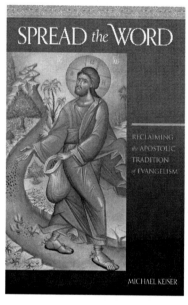

A Beginner's Guide to Prayer
The Orthodox Way to Draw Closer to God

This is a book for those struggling to establish an effective life of prayer. Written neither for seasoned monastic nor lofty scholar, *A Beginner's Guide to Prayer* speaks to the average man or woman on the street who desires a deeper relationship with God but is unsure how or where to begin. Drawing from nearly 2000 years of Orthodox spiritual wisdom, the author offers warm, practical, pastoral advice whose genius is to be found in its homespun simplicity and straightforwardness of style.

If you've been desiring to make prayer a meaningful and regular part of your life, *A Beginner's Guide to Prayer* will help set you on your way. But be careful—prayer can be habit-forming! In fact, the advice offered in this book may just change the course of the rest of your life. So, in the words of the author, "What are you waiting for? Start to pray!"

Paperback, 104 pages (ISBN 978-1-888212-64-8)

CP Order No. 006077—$10.95

Spread the Word
Reclaiming the Apostolic Tradition of Evangelism

Does "Orthodox evangelism" sound like an oxymoron? It shouldn't. The Orthodox Church has an unbroken tradition of evangelism that goes back to the Apostles. But Orthodox evangelism does look rather different from the Protestant variety.

With his characteristic straightforward and humorous style, Fr. Michael Keiser covers the history of Orthodox evangelism, the rationale and the methods for continuing this tradition in our contemporary Western post-Christian society.

Paperback, 216 pages (ISBN: 978-1-936270-09-5)

CP Order No. 008101—$17.95

Books on Spirituality & Worship from Conciliar Press

Everywhere Present
Christianity in a One-Storey Universe
by Fr. Stephen Freeman

Have you ever referred to God as "the Man upstairs"? Most Christians living in a secular society have unwittingly relegated God and all things spiritual to the "second storey" of the universe: a realm we cannot reach except through death. The effect of this is to banish God, along with the saints and angels, from our everyday lives.

In *Everywhere Present,* popular blogger and podcaster Fr. Stephen Freeman makes a compelling case for becoming aware of God's living and active presence in every moment of our lives here and now. Learning to practice your Christian faith in a one-storey universe will change your life—and make possible the living, intimate relationship with God you've always dreamed of.

A Book of Hours
Meditations on the Traditional Christian Hours of Prayer
by Patricia Colling Egan

Eastern and Western Christians share a rich spiritual heritage in the Hours of Prayer—the brief services of praise and psalmody that mark the progress of each day, sanctifying the hours of our lives. In this gem of a book, Patricia Egan digs deeply into the meaning of each of the Hours, drawing on poetry, nature, experience, and theology to show how the services reflect the different aspects of our salvation and our lives. *A Book of Hours* is an excellent companion for anyone who wants to experience the blessing of praying through the Hours of each day.

Bread & Water, Wine & Oil
An Orthodox Christian Experience of God
by Fr. Meletios Webber

Worry, despair, insecurity, fear of death . . . these are our daily companions. It is precisely where we hurt most that the experience of the Orthodox Church has much to offer. The remedy is not any simple admonitions to fight the good fight, cheer up, or think positively. Rather, the Orthodox method is to change the way we look at the human person (starting with ourselves). Orthodoxy shows us how to "be transformed by the renewing of our mind"—a process that is aided by participation in the traditional ascetic practices and Mysteries of the Church. In this unique and accessible book, Archimandrite Meletios Webber first explores the role of mystery in the Christian life, then walks the reader through the seven major Mysteries (or sacraments) of the Orthodox Church, showing the way to a richer, fuller life in Christ.

Let Us Attend
A Journey Through the Orthodox Divine Liturgy
by Father Lawrence Farley

Esteemed author and Scripture commentator Fr. Lawrence Farley provides a guide to understanding the Divine Liturgy, and a vibrant reminder of the centrality of the Eucharist in living the Christian life.

Every Sunday morning we are literally taken on a journey into the Kingdom of God. Fr. Lawrence guides believers in a devotional and historical walk through the Orthodox Liturgy. Examining the Liturgy section by section, he provides both historical explanations of how the Liturgy evolved and devotional insights aimed at helping us pray the Liturgy in the way the Fathers intended. In better understanding the depth of the Liturgy's meaning and purpose, we can pray it properly. If you would like a deeper understanding of your Sunday morning experience so that you can draw closer to God, then this book is for you.

The Jesus Prayer
A Gift from the Fathers
by Fr. David Hester

"O Lord Jesus Christ, Son of God, have mercy on me." This prayer has been on the lips of Christians since the time of the Desert Fathers. What is its history? How do we make it our own? This booklet traces the development of the Jesus Prayer through the early centuries of the Church and follows its progression through Mount Athos, the teachings of St. Gregory Palamas and others, and discusses its modern revival in the 19th and 20th centuries. Concludes with a brief discussion of how this prayer can be appropriated by the individual believer today.

Mary, Worthy of All Praise
Reflections on the Virgin Mary
by Fr. David Smith

In the Gospel of Luke, we hear the angel's timeless proclamation to Mary, "Rejoice, highly favored one, the Lord is with you; blessed are you among women" (Luke 1:28). Every generation of Christians must contemplate these angelic words, for Mary is the Theotokos and Mother of our Lord. Every culture must confront her mystery. Through its worship services, the Church gives us many opportunities to consider the place of the Mother of Jesus Christ in our lives. The Paraklesis service, sung every day during the Virgin's Lent, offers the perfect vehicle to do just that. Sung from the first to the fifteenth of August, and at other times of illness and distress, the Paraklesis is a supplicatory song, a canon of praise, a series of poems celebrating with honor the Mother of Jesus our Lord. Fr. David Smith shares with us his own personal meditations on Mary, based upon his reflections on the Paraklesis service.

Turning the Heart to God
by St. Theophan the Recluse
translated by Fr. Kenneth Kaisch and Igumen Iona Zhiltsov

One of the most profound works on repentance in all of Christendom. St. Theophan, a beloved Orthodox bishop from nineteenth-century Russia, speaks not only from a deep knowledge of the Church Fathers, but also from a lifetime of experience in turning his heart to God—and guiding others on this glorious Way that leads to our salvation. His writings are unique in that he combines centuries of Church wisdom with keen psychological insights for us today.

Repentance is not a popular term here in the West, yet it is the cornerstone of the Lord's gospel, and the entrance into God's kingdom. *Turning the Heart to God* is a manual of true spiritual transformation in a world of often cheap grace . . . a classic book that has the power to change our lives, if we let it.

Introductory Books on the Orthodox Church

What Is the Orthodox Church?
by Fr. Marc Dunaway (Published by Conciliar Press)

Examines the unbroken apostolic chain linking past to present in the historic Church. Written by a former evangelical pastor whose study of the biblical and historical evidence supporting this very doctrine led him to chrismation and finally ordination in the two-thousand-year-old Orthodox Church.

The Orthodox Church
by Bishop Kallistos Ware (Published by Penguin)

This classic introductory work on the Orthodox Church has become a worldwide standard in colleges and seminaries. Part One describes the history of the Orthodox Church. Part Two outlines Orthodox doctrine and worship.

The final chapter deals with restoring the breaches between East and West.

The Orthodox Faith (4 volumes)
by Father Thomas Hopko
(Published by Orthodox Christian Publication Center)
An introductory handbook on Orthodox faith and life. Volume 1: *Doctrine/* Volume 2: *Worship/* Volume 3: *Bible and Church History/* Volume 4: *Spirituality*. Presented in brief chapters, this handbook series is excellent for quick reference or study, and provides valuable teaching material for both teens and adults.

Introducing the Orthodox Church
by Father Anthony Coniaris (Published by Light & Life)
Fr. Coniaris provides his readers with an invaluable introduction to the beliefs, practices, and patterns of Orthodox Christianity. Written in a popular and easy-to-read style, *Introducing the Orthodox Church* touches all the important bases without sacrificing balance or accuracy.

The Orthodox Way
by Bishop Kallistos Ware
(Published by St. Vladimir's Seminary Press)
An excellent companion to *The Orthodox Church*, this book discusses the spiritual life of the Christian and sets forth the basic issues of theology as a way of life for the follower of Christ.

Orthodox Worship
by Williams & Anstall (Published by Light & Life)
Discusses the living continuity between the worship of Judaism (temple and synagogue worship) and that of the early Church, as well as the origins of the Orthodox liturgy.

The Orthodox Church: 455 Questions & Answers
by Father Stanley Harakas (Published by Light & Life)
A comprehensive handbook, indexed with easy cross-referencing. Answers 455 questions most asked about the history, doctrine, and practice of the Orthodox Church.

To request a Conciliar Press catalog, to obtain current pricing or ordering information, or to place a credit card order, **please call Conciliar Press at (800) 967-7377 or (219) 728-22168, or log onto our website: www.conciliarpress.com**

Conciliar Media Ministries hopes you have enjoyed and benefited from this book. The proceeds from the sales of our books only partially cover the costs of operating our nonprofit ministry—which includes both the work of **Conciliar Press** and the work of **Ancient Faith Radio.** Your financial support makes it possible to continue this ministry both in print and online. Donations are tax-deductible and can be made at www.ancientfaith.com.

 ANCIENT FAITH RADIO

Internet-Based Orthodox Radio:
Podcasts, 24-hour music and talk stations,
teaching, conference recordings, and much more,
at www.ancientfaith.com

CPSIA information can be obtained at www.ICGtesting.com
Printed in the USA
LVOW041150011211

257338LV00001B/13/P